SIDE *by* SIDES

P R E S T W I C K   H O U S E ,   I N C .

THE
TAMING
OF THE
SHREW

WILLIAM SHAKESPEARE

Shakespeare's text

on the left;

modern rendering

on the right

PRESTWICK
H O U S E
INCORPORATED

P.O. Box 658 • Clayton, DE 19938
Tel: 1.800.932.4593
Web site: www.prestwickhouse.com

ISBN: 978-1-58049-521-9

Table of Contents

DRAMATIS PERSONAE

A Lord.
CHRISTOPHER SLY, a beggar
HOSTESS, PAGE, PLAYERS, HUNTSMEN,
  and SERVANTS.
} Persons in the Induction.

BAPTISTA, a rich gentleman of Padua.

VINCENTIO, an old gentleman of Pisa.

LUCENTIO, son to VINCENTIO, in love with Bianca.

PETRUCHIO, a gentleman of Verona, a suitor to Katherine.

GREMIO
HORTENSIO
} suitors to Bianca.

TRANIO
BIONDELLO
} servants to Lucentio.

GRUMIO
CURTIS
} servants to Petruchio.

A PEDANT (TEACHER)

KATHERINE, the shrew
BIANCA
} daughters to Baptista.

WIDOW

TAILOR, HABERDASHER, and SERVANTS attending on BAPTISTA and
  PETRUCHIO.

SCENE: *Padua, and PETRUCHIO's country house.*

INDUCTION

SCENE 1
Before an alehouse on a heath.

[Enter Hostess and Sly]

SLY: I'll pheeze you, in faith.

HOS: A pair of stocks, you rogue!

SLY: Ye are a baggage: the Slys are no rogues; look in the chroni-
cles; we came in with Richard Conqueror. Therefore paucas
pallabris; let the world slide: sessa!

HOS: You will not pay for the glasses you have burst?

SLY: No, not a denier. Go by, Jeronimy: go to thy cold bed, and
warm thee.

HOS: I know my remedy; I must go fetch the third-borough.
[Exit]

SLY: Third, or fourth, or fifth borough, I'll answer him by law:
I'll not budge an inch, boy: let him come, and kindly.
[Falls asleep]

[Horns winded. Enter a Lord from hunting, with his train]

LOR: Huntsman, I charge thee, tender well my hounds:
Breathe Merriman, the poor cur is emboss'd;

5

10

INDUCTION

SCENE 1
Before a tavern on a hill.

[Hostess and Sly enter]

SLY: *I'll beat you, I swear.*

HOSTESS: *You'll be put in the stocks, you rogue!*

SLY: *You're a hag. The Slys aren't rogues. Look in the history books; we came here with Richard the Conqueror. So, stop talking, let the world pass by, and be quiet!*

HOSTESS: *You won't pay for the glasses you've broken?*

SLY: *No, not a cent. Get out of here, by St. Jerome; go jump in the bed you never sleep in!*

HOSTESS: *I know where I can get some help. I'll go get the third sheriff.*
[Hostess exits]

SLY: *Get the third or fourth or fifth sheriff; I'll give him a lawful answer. I won't move an inch. Boy, let him come; I welcome it.*

[Sly falls asleep. Some horns blow. A Lord enters with his hunting party]

LORD: *Hunter, I order you to take good care of my dogs. My poor dog, Merriman, is foaming at the mouth. And put Clowder with him. Did you*

7

And couple Clowder with the deep-mouth'd brach.
15   Saw'st thou not, boy, how Silver made it good
At the hedge-corner, in the coldest fault?
I would not lose the dog for twenty pound.

1ST HUN: Why, Belman is as good as he, my lord;
He cried upon it at the merest loss
20   And twice to-day pick'd out the dullest scent:
Trust me, I take him for the better dog.

LOR: Thou art a fool: if Echo were as fleet,
I would esteem him worth a dozen such.
But sup them well and look unto them all:
25   To-morrow I intend to hunt again.

1ST HUN: I will, my lord.

LOR: What's here? one dead, or drunk? See, doth he breathe?

2ND HUN: He breathes, my lord. Were he not warm'd with ale,
This were a bed but cold to sleep so soundly.

30   LOR: O monstrous beast! how like a swine he lies!
Grim death, how foul and loathsome is thine image!
Sirs, I will practise on this drunken man.
What think you, if he were convey'd to bed,
Wrapp'd in sweet clothes, rings put upon his fingers,
35   A most delicious banquet by his bed,
And brave attendants near him when he wakes,
Would not the beggar then forget himself?

1ST HUN: Believe me, lord, I think he cannot choose.

2ND HUN: It would seem strange unto him when he waked.

40   LOR: Even as a flattering dream or worthless fancy.
Then take him up and manage well the jest:
Carry him gently to my fairest chamber

see, boy, how Silver tracked that rabbit into the hedge when the others lost the scent? I would not trade that dog for twenty silver pieces.

FIRST HUNTER: Belman is as good as Silver, my lord. He barked when the others didn't and twice today he picked out the scent of the rabbit. Trust me, I believe he is the better dog.

LORD: You are a fool. If Echo were as fast, I would consider him worth a dozen Belmans. But feed them well and look after them all; tomorrow I intend to hunt again.

FIRST HUNTER: I will, my lord.

LORD: Who's this, someone who is dead or drunk? Look, is he breathing?

SECOND HUNTER: He is breathing, my lord. If he had not drunk so much beer, he would not be sleeping so soundly on the floor.

LORD: He's like a monster! He's like a pig lying there! He looks like foul and ugly death itself! Sirs, let's play a trick on this drunk man. What would you say if we put him to bed, put fancy clothing on him and rings on his fingers, fine food by his bed and servants nearby? Do you think when he wakes up he'll forget that he's a beggar?

FIRST HUNTER: Believe me, lord, I think he won't be able to tell.

SECOND HUNTER: It will seem strange to him when he wakes up.

LORD: It will be like a good dream or a meaningless daydream. Pick him up and fool him well. Carry him gently to my bedroom and put erotic pictures on the walls. Bathe his clammy head in warm distilled water and

And hang it round with all my wanton pictures:
Balm his foul head in warm distilled waters
45   And burn sweet wood to make the lodging sweet:
Procure me music ready when he wakes,
To make a dulcet and a heavenly sound;
And if he chance to speak, be ready straight
And with a low submissive reverence
50   Say 'What is it your honour will command?'
Let one attend him with a silver basin
Full of rose-water and bestrew'd with flowers,
Another bear the ewer, the third a diaper,
And say 'Will't please your lordship cool your hands?'
55   Some one be ready with a costly suit
And ask him what apparel he will wear;
Another tell him of his hounds and horse,
And that his lady mourns at his disease:
Persuade him that he hath been lunatic;
60   And when he says he is, say that he dreams,
For he is nothing but a mighty lord.
This do and do it kindly, gentle sirs:
It will be pastime passing excellent,
If it be husbanded with modesty.

65 1ST HUN: My lord, I warrant you we will play our part,
As he shall think by our true diligence
He is no less than what we say he is.

LOR: Take him up gently and to bed with him;
And each one to his office when he wakes.
                        [Some bear out Sly. A trumpet sounds]
70   Sirrah, go see what trumpet 'tis that sounds:
                                [Exit Servingman]
Belike, some noble gentleman that means,
Travelling some journey, to repose him here.

[Re-enter Servingman]
How now! who is it?

burn incense to make the room smell sweet. Make sure to have sweet and heavenly music ready when he wakes up and, if he speaks, be ready to say with a low voice like a servant, "What would you like, your honor?" Let one person stand there with a silver bowl full of rose water and flower petals; have another hold the pitcher and a third a soft cloth, and say, "Would your lordship like to cool his hands?" Someone be ready with an expensive suit and ask what clothing he will wear. Have another tell him about his hunting dogs and horse, and that his lady is worried about his disease. Convince him that he has been crazy and when he says he is, say that he is only dreaming, for he is really a mighty lord. Do this and do it kindly, gentle sirs. It will be an excellent way to pass the time if we do it carefully and well.

FIRST HUNTER: *My lord, I promise you we will play our part, so that he will think, by our hard work, that he is what we say he is.*

LORD: *Pick him up gently and put him to bed, and each of you play your parts well when he wakes up.* [Some of them take him away. A trumpet sounds] *Sir, go see what that trumpeting is about.* [Servant exits] *It is probably some noble gentleman who is travelling and wants to stay here at the tavern.*

[Servant re-enters]
Come on! Who is it that has arrived?

11

SER: An't please your honour, players
75   That offer service to your lordship.

LOR: Bid them come near.

[Enter Players]
        Now, fellows, you are welcome.

PLAYERS: We thank your honour.

LOR: Do you intend to stay with me tonight?

80   A PLAYER: So please your lordship to accept our duty.

LOR: With all my heart. This fellow I remember,
        Since once he play'd a farmer's eldest son:
        'Twas where you woo'd the gentlewoman so well:
        I have forgot your name; but, sure, that part
85   Was aptly fitted and naturally perform'd.

A PLAYER: I think 'twas Soto that your honour means.

LOR: 'Tis very true: thou didst it excellent.
        Well, you are come to me in happy time;
        The rather for I have some sport in hand
90   Wherein your cunning can assist me much.
        There is a lord will hear you play to-night:
        But I am doubtful of your modesties;
        Lest over-eyeing of his odd behavior,—
        For yet his honour never heard a play—
95   You break into some merry passion
        And so offend him; for I tell you, sirs,
        If you should smile he grows impatient.

A PLAYER: Fear not, my lord: we can contain ourselves,
        Were he the veriest antic in the world.

100 LOR: Go, sirrah, take them to the buttery,

SERVANT: *If it doesn't offend you, my lord, it is some players who have come to offer their services to you.*

LORD: *Tell them to come here.*

[The Players enter]
  Now, fellows, you are welcome.

PLAYERS: *We thank you, your honor.*

LORD: *Do you intend to stay with me tonight?*

A PLAYER: *If you would like us to stay and play for you, my lord.*

LORD: *With all my heart. This fellow I remember because he once played a farmer's oldest son. You wooed a woman well in the scene. I have forgotten your name, but that part you played suited you well and was performed excellently.*

A PLAYER: *I think it was the part of Soto that your honor means.*

LORD: *Yes! That's right! You played it excellently. Well, you have showed up at just the right time because I have a trick that I want to play, and your skills in acting can help me achieve it. There is a lord that will hear you play tonight, but I am worried that you might lose control when you see how strangely he acts. This lord has never seen a play, and I'm afraid you might offend him if you laugh at the way he acts. I have to tell you, sirs, if you so much as smile, he will lose his temper.*

A PLAYER: *Don't be afraid, my lord. We could keep a straight face even if he were the biggest buffoon in the world.*

LORD: *Go, sir, and take the players to my kitchen, and feed them well and*

And give them friendly welcome every one:
Let them want nothing that my house affords.

[Exit one with the Players]

Sirrah, go you to Barthol'mew my page,
And see him dress'd in all suits like a lady:

105   That done, conduct him to the drunkard's chamber;
And call him 'madam,' do him obeisance.
Tell him from me, as he will win my love,
He bear himself with honourable action,
Such as he hath observed in noble ladies

110   Unto their lords, by them accomplished:
Such duty to the drunkard let him do
With soft low tongue and lowly courtesy,
And say 'What is't your honour will command,
Wherein your lady and your humble wife

115   May show her duty and make known her love?'
And then with kind embracements, tempting kisses,
And with declining head into his bosom,
Bid him shed tears, as being overjoy'd
To see her noble lord restored to health,

120   Who for this seven years hath esteem'd him
No better than a poor and loathsome beggar:
And if the boy have not a woman's gift
To rain a shower of commanded tears,
An onion will do well for such a shift,

125   Which in a napkin being close convey'd
Shall in despite enforce a watery eye.
See this dispatch'd with all the haste thou canst:
Anon I'll give thee more instructions.

[Exit a Servingman]

I know the boy will well usurp the grace,

130   Voice, gait and action of a gentlewoman:
I long to hear him call the drunkard husband,
And how my men will stay themselves from laughter
When they do homage to this simple peasant.
I'll in to counsel them; haply my presence

135   May well abate the over-merry spleen
Which otherwise would grow into extremes.   *[Exeunt]*

make them feel at home; anything that is mine is theirs. [A Servant exits with the Players] *Sir, you go to Bartholomew, my page, and dress him up like a lady. Then take him to the drunk man's room and call him "madam" and obey his orders. Tell Bartholomew that I said I will be very happy if he plays the part like the honorable noble ladies he has seen with their lords. Tell him to use a quiet voice with the drunk and be very kind and say, "What is it your honor will have his lady and his humble wife do to show her love to him?" And then with kind hugs, tempting kisses, and laying his head on his chest, tell him to cry as if he were overjoyed to see his noble lord restored to health after seven years of thinking that he was nothing more than a poor and loathsome beggar. And if Bartholomew is not able to cry on command like a woman can, tell him to put a slice of onion in a handkerchief and hold it close enough to bring tears to his eyes. Make sure you do this as quickly as you can. I'll give you more instructions later.* [A Servant exits]

I know Bartholomew will portray the grace, voice, walk, and actions of a gentlewoman well. I long to hear him call the drunk man husband and see how my men will keep from laughing when they pretend to be the servants of this peasant. I will go in and coach them so that perhaps my presence will keep them from laughing too much at the joke and giving it away.

[All exit]

SCENE 2
A bedchamber in the Lord's house.

[Enter aloft Sly, with Attendants; some with apparel, others with basin and ewer and appurtenances; and Lord]

SLY: For God's sake, a pot of small ale.

1ST SER: Will't please your lordship drink a cup of sack?

2ND SER: Will't please your honour taste of these conserves?

3RD SER: What raiment will your honour wear to-day?

5   SLY: I am Christophero Sly; call not me 'honour' nor 'lordship': I
ne'er drank sack in my life; and if you give me any conserves,
give me conserves of beef: ne'er ask me what raiment I'll
wear; for I have no more doublets than backs, no more stockings than legs, nor no more shoes than feet; nay, sometimes
10   more feet than shoes, or such shoes as my toes look through
the over-leather.

LOR: Heaven cease this idle humour in your honour!
O, that a mighty man of such descent,
Of such possessions and so high esteem,
15   Should be infused with so foul a spirit!

SLY: What, would you make me mad? Am not I Christopher Sly,
old Sly's son of Burtonheath, by birth a pedlar, by education a
cardmaker, by transmutation a bear-herd, and now by present
profession a tinker? Ask Marian Hacket, the fat ale-wife of
20   Wincot, if she know me not: if she say I am not fourteen
pence on the score for sheer ale, score me up for the lyingest
knave in Christendom. What! I am not bestraught: here's—

3RD SER: O, this it is that makes your lady mourn!

SCENE 2
A bedroom in the Lord's house.

[Enter Sly, with Attendants; some with clothing, others with a basin and pitcher and other objects of a rich man's household; and the Lord]

SLY: *For God's sake, a glass of beer!*

FIRST SERVANT: *Wouldn't your honor prefer some wine?*

SECOND SERVANT: *Would it please your lordship to taste these fancy candied fruits?*

THIRD SERVANT: *What clothing will your honor wear today?*

SLY: *I am Christophero Sly. Don't call me 'honor' or 'lordship.' I never drank wine in my life. And if you give me candied anything, give me candied beef. Don't ask me what clothing I'll wear. I have no more shirts than I have backs, no more stockings than I have legs, and no more shoes than I have feet. Well, no, sometimes I have more feet than I have shoes, and sometimes I have such bad shoes that my toes poke out through the leather.*

LORD: *Oh, may heaven stop this terrible ranting of your honor! It is terrible that a man of your background, with such fine possessions and being so well respected, should be filled with such a foul spirit!*

SLY: *What, are you trying to make me crazy? Am I not Christopher Sly, old Sly's son of Burtonheath village, who was born a peddler, taught to be a wool-comber, turned into a bear-keeper, and now in my present job a pot-mender? Ask Marian Hacket, the fat tavern keeper's wife from Wincot, if she knows me. If she doesn't say I owe her fourteen pence for beer, call me the biggest liar in the Christian world. What! I am not crazy, here's–*

THIRD SERVANT: *Oh, this kind of talk is what makes your lady so unhappy!*

17

2ND SER: O, this is it that makes your servants droop!

LOR: Hence comes it that your kindred shuns your house,
25   As beaten hence by your strange lunacy.
     O noble lord, bethink thee of thy birth,
     Call home thy ancient thoughts from banishment
     And banish hence these abject lowly dreams.
     Look how thy servants do attend on thee,
30   Each in his office ready at thy beck.
     Wilt thou have music? hark! Apollo plays,   *[Music]*
     And twenty caged nightingales do sing:
     Or wilt thou sleep? we'll have thee to a couch
     Softer and sweeter than the lustful bed
35   On purpose trimm'd up for Semiramis.
     Say thou wilt walk; we will bestrew the ground:
     Or wilt thou ride? thy horses shall be trapp'd,
     Their harness studded all with gold and pearl.
     Dost thou love hawking? thou hast hawks will soar
40   Above the morning lark: or wilt thou hunt?
     Thy hounds shall make the welkin answer them
     And fetch shrill echoes from the hollow earth.

1ST SER: Say thou wilt course; thy greyhounds are as swift
     As breathed stags, ay, fleeter than the roe.

45 2ND SER: Dost thou love pictures? we will fetch thee straight
     Adonis painted by a running brook,
     And Cytherea all in sedges hid,
     Which seem to move and wanton with her breath,
     Even as the waving sedges play with wind.

50 LOR: We'll show thee Io as she was a maid,
     And how she was beguiled and surprised,
     As lively painted as the deed was done.

3RD SER: Or Daphne roaming through a thorny wood,
     Scratching her legs that one shall swear she bleeds,

SECOND SERVANT: *This kind of talk is what makes your servants faint!*

LORD: *This is why your family stays away from you; they are beaten away by your strange lunacy. Oh, noble lord, remember your noble birth, remember where you came from, and get rid of these strange thoughts of being a peasant. Look how your servants wait on you; each one is ready to do whatever you ask. Will you have some music? Listen! It is like Apollo, the god of music, is playing and twenty caged nightingales are singing. Will you sleep? We'll take you to a couch that is softer and sweeter than the well-trimmed bed of the lusty Queen Semiramis. If you walk, we will cover the ground with reeds. If you ride, we will bring your horses with the gold and pearl harnesses. Do you love hunting with hawks? You have hawks that will soar above the morning lark. Or will you hunt? Your hounds will make the sky answer them, and their barking will make shrill echoes on the earth.*

FIRST SERVANT: *Let's say you will hunt; your greyhounds are as swift as the swiftest stags, yes, faster than the deer.*

SECOND SERVANT: *Do you love paintings? We'll bring you a painting of Adonis by a running brook and Venus hiding in the reeds that will seem to move and breathe, just like the reeds that sway with the wind.*

LORD: *We'll show you Io when she was a maid, and how she was tricked and surprised. It will be as lively a painting as the deed itself was.*

THIRD SERVANT: *How about a picture of Daphne roaming through thorny woods, with such scratches on her legs that you'll swear she is bleeding,*

55   And at that sight shall sad Apollo weep,
So workmanly the blood and tears are drawn.

LOR: Thou art a lord, and nothing but a lord:
Thou hast a lady far more beautiful
Than any woman in this waning age.

60   1ST SER: And till the tears that she hath shed for thee
Like envious floods o'er-run her lovely face,
She was the fairest creature in the world;
And yet she is inferior to none.

SLY: Am I a lord? and have I such a lady?
65   Or do I dream? or have I dream'd till now?
I do not sleep: I see, I hear, I speak;
I smell sweet savours and I feel soft things:
Upon my life, I am a lord indeed
And not a tinker nor Christophero Sly.
70   Well, bring our lady hither to our sight;
And once again, a pot o' the smallest ale.

2ND SER: Will't please your mightiness to wash your hands?
O, how we joy to see your wit restored!
O, that once more you knew but what you are!
75   These fifteen years you have been in a dream;
Or when you waked, so waked as if you slept.

SLY: These fifteen years! by my fay, a goodly nap.
But did I never speak of all that time?

1ST SER: O, yes, my lord, but very idle words:
80   For though you lay here in this goodly chamber,
Yet would you say ye were beaten out of door;
And rail upon the hostess of the house;
And say you would present her at the leet,
Because she brought stone jugs and no seal'd quarts:
85   Sometimes you would call out for Cicely Hacket.

and even sad Apollo will weep at the sight, because the blood and tears are so well drawn.

LORD: You are a lord, and nothing but a lord. You have a lady far more beautiful than any woman in this century.

FIRST SERVANT: Even though the tears that she cries for you overrun her lovely face like a flood, she is still the fairest creature in the world and inferior to no one.

SLY: Am I a lord and do I have such a lady or am I dreaming? Or have I been dreaming until now? I do not sleep. I see, I hear, I speak; I smell sweet smells and I feel soft things. It's true, I really am a lord and not a pot-mender or Christopher Sly. Well, bring my lady here, let me see her; and once again, bring me a glass of beer.

SECOND SERVANT: Will it please your mightiness to wash your hands? Oh, how joyful we are to see your memory returned, now that you know truly what you are! For fifteen years you have been in a dream; or when you were awake, it was like you were sleeping.

SLY: For fifteen years! Oh, my goodness, that's quite a nap. But I never spoke during all that time?

FIRST SERVANT: Oh, yes, my lord, but very foolish words. Even though you were here in this room, you would say you were beaten outdoors, and you would yell at the hostess of the house and say you would take her to court because she was trying to cheat you with uneven stone jugs instead of equal-sized quart bottles. Sometimes, you would call out for Cicely Hacket.

SLY: Ay, the woman's maid of the house.

3RD SER: Why, sir, you know no house nor no such maid,
Nor no such men as you have reckon'd up,
As Stephen Sly and old John Naps of Greece
90 And Peter Turph and Henry Pimpernell
And twenty more such names and men as these
Which never were nor no man ever saw.

SLY: Now Lord be thanked for my good amends!

ALL: Amen.

95 SLY: I thank thee: thou shalt not lose by it.

[Enter the Page as a lady, with attendants]

PAGE: How fares my noble lord?

SLY: Marry, I fare well, for here is cheer enough.
Where is my wife?

PAGE: Here, noble lord: what is thy will with her?

100 SLY: Are you my wife and will not call me husband?
My men should call me 'lord': I am your goodman.

PAGE: My husband and my lord, my lord and husband;
I am your wife in all obedience.

SLY: I know it well. What must I call her?

105 LOR: Madam.

SLY: Al'ce madam, or Joan madam?

LOR: 'Madam,' and nothing else: so lords call ladies.

22

SLY: *Yes, the woman's maid of the house.*

THIRD SERVANT: *Why, sir, you don't know that house or that maid, or any of the men you called out to, like Stephen Sly and John Naps of Greece, and Peter Turph and Henry Pimpernell and twenty more names of men that never existed and nobody ever saw.*

SLY: *Now the lord be thanked for my good return to health!*

ALL: *Amen.*

SLY: *I thank you. You will be well paid for it.*

[The Page enters dressed as a lady, with attendants]

PAGE: *How is my noble lord feeling?*

SLY: *Indeed, I feel well enough, for here is cheer enough. Where is my wife?*

PAGE: *Here, noble lord, what do you want with her?*

SLY: *Are you my wife and won't call me husband? My men call me lord; I am your husband.*

PAGE: *My husband and my lord, my lord and husband; I am your wife in all obedience.*

SLY: *Yes, I know.* [To the LORD, not sure of what his wife's name is] *What should I call her?*

LORD: *Madam.*

SLY: *Alice madam or Joan madam?*

LORD: *"Madam," and nothing else. That is what lords call ladies.*

SLY: Madam wife, they say that I have dream'd
       And slept above some fifteen year or more.

110 PAG: Ay, and the time seems thirty unto me,
           Being all this time abandon'd from your bed.

     SLY: 'Tis much. Servants, leave me and her alone.
           Madam, undress you and come now to bed.

     PAG: Thrice noble lord, let me entreat of you
115   To pardon me yet for a night or two,
           Or, if not so, until the sun be set:
           For your physicians have expressly charged,
           In peril to incur your former malady,
           That I should yet absent me from your bed:
120   I hope this reason stands for my excuse.

     SLY: Ay, it stands so that I may hardly tarry so long. But I would
           be loath to fall into my dreams again: I will therefore tarry in
           despite of the flesh and the blood.

     [Enter a Messenger]

     MESS: Your honour's players, hearing your amendment,
125   Are come to play a pleasant comedy;
           For so your doctors hold it very meet,
           Seeing too much sadness hath congeal'd your blood,
           And melancholy is the nurse of frenzy:
           Therefore they thought it good you hear a play
130   And frame your mind to mirth and merriment,
           Which bars a thousand harms and lengthens life.

     SLY: Marry, I will, let them play it. Is not a comondy a Christmas
           gambold or a tumbling-trick?

     PAG: No, my good lord; it is more pleasing stuff.

135 SLY: What, household stuff?

24

SLY: *Madam wife, they say that I have dreamed and slept more than fifteen years.*

PAGE: *Yes, and it seems like thirty years to me, since we have not been in bed together all this time.*

SLY: *That is a long time. Servants, leave us alone. Madam, get undressed and come to bed.*

PAGE: *My very noble lord, I ask that we wait a night or two, or, if not that, at least until the sun goes down. Your doctors have given me instructions that I should not go to bed with you yet, or your sickness may return. Although it is difficult, I hope you understand.*

SLY: *Yes, it is hard to understand, but I don't want to fall into my dreams again. I will take things slowly even though my flesh and my blood tell me not to.*

[A Messenger enters]

MESSENGER: *Your honor's players, hearing of your return to health, have come to play a pleasant comedy. Your doctors think it is a good idea, because sadness has congealed your blood, and melancholy makes the craziness return. Therefore, they thought it was a good idea for you to hear a play that would bring you mirth and merriment, which keeps away a thousand harmful things and makes you live longer.*

SLY: *Indeed, I will; let them play it. Is it a comedy, a Christmas play, or some acrobatics?*

PAGE: *No, my good lord; it is more pleasing stuff.*

SLY: *What, a play about furniture?*

PAG: It is a kind of history.

SLY: Well, we'll see't. Come, madam wife, sit by my side and let
the world slip: we shall ne'er be younger.

[Flourish]

❦

PAGE: *It is a kind of history.*

SLY: *Well, we'll see it. Come, madam wife, sit by my side, and let the world pass by. We will never be younger.*

[A trumpet sounds]

ACT 1

Scene 1
Padua. A public place.

[Enter Lucentio and his man Tranio]

Luc: Tranio, since for the great desire I had
       To see fair Padua, nursery of arts,
       I am arrived for fruitful Lombardy,
       The pleasant garden of great Italy;
5   And by my father's love and leave am arm'd
       With his good will and thy good company,
       My trusty servant, well approved in all,
       Here let us breathe and haply institute
       A course of learning and ingenious studies.
10   Pisa renown'd for grave citizens
       Gave me my being and my father first,
       A merchant of great traffic through the world,
       Vincentio come of Bentivolii.
       Vincentio's son, brought up in Florence,
15   It shall become to serve all hopes conceived,
       To deck his fortune with his virtuous deeds:
       And therefore, Tranio, for the time I study,
       Virtue and that part of philosophy
       Will I apply that treats of happiness
20   By virtue specially to be achieved.
       Tell me thy mind; for I have Pisa left
       And am to Padua come, as he that leaves
       A shallow plash to plunge him in the deep
       And with satiety seeks to quench his thirst.

ACT I

SCENE 1
Padua. A public place.

[Lucentio and his servant Tranio enter]

LUCENTIO: *Tranio, because I wanted to see fair Padua, the birthplace of the arts, I got my father's loving permission to come with you, my trusty servant, to prosperous Lombardy, known to all as the pleasant garden of great Italy. Let's rest here and start a course of learning and ingenious studies. I was born in Pisa, known for its serious citizens, and my father, Vincentio Bentivolii, a great merchant in the world, brought me up in Florence. Therefore, Tranio, for the time being, I will study virtue and philosophy; for only by living virtuously can a person be happy. Tell me what you think, Tranio, for I have left Pisa and come to Padua, like a person who goes from a shallow puddle to the deep sea to drink his fill and quench his deep thirst.*

25   Tra: *Mi perdonato*, gentle master mine,
         I am in all affected as yourself;
         Glad that you thus continue your resolve
         To suck the sweets of sweet philosophy.
         Only, good master, while we do admire
30   This virtue and this moral discipline,
         Let's be no stoics nor no stocks, I pray;
         Or so devote to Aristotle's cheques
         As Ovid be an outcast quite abjured:
         Balk logic with acquaintance that you have
35   And practise rhetoric in your common talk;
         Music and poesy use to quicken you;
         The mathematics and the metaphysics,
         Fall to them as you find your stomach serves you;
         No profit grows where is no pleasure ta'en:
40   In brief, sir, study what you most affect.

   Luc: Gramercies, Tranio, well dost thou advise.
         If, Biondello, thou wert come ashore,
         We could at once put us in readiness,
         And take a lodging fit to entertain
45   Such friends as time in Padua shall beget.
         But stay a while: what company is this?

   Tra: Master, some show to welcome us to town.

[Enter Baptista, Katherine, Bianca, Gremio, and Hortensio. Lucentio and Tranio stand by]

   Bap: Gentlemen, importune me no farther,
         For how I firmly am resolved you know;
50   That is, not bestow my youngest daughter
         Before I have a husband for the elder:
         If either of you both love Katherine,
         Because I know you well and love you well,
         Leave shall you have to court her at your pleasure.

55   Gre: *[Aside]* To cart her rather: she's too rough for me.
         There, there, Hortensio, will you any wife?

TRANIO: Pardon me, gentle master mine, I am just as affected by this as you, and glad that you continue your determination to suck the sweet cream from the top of the milkjug of philosophy. But, good master, while I admire virtue and morality, let's not be too rigorous or blockheaded about it. Let's not so devote ourselves to Aristotle's philosophic restraints that we become outcasts like Ovid. Let's not talk chopped-logic and fancy rhetoric with our friends. Music and poetry can make you full of life; math and metaphysics you can study as you see fit. You cannot profit from study and rigor if you don't take the time to have some fun, too! In brief, sir, study the things you like.

LUCENTIO: Many thanks, Tranio, you advise me well. If Biondello were here, we could get ready at once, and find a place to live and entertain the new friends we make in Padua. Hold on, who is this?

TRANIO: Master, it is some show to welcome us to town.

[Baptista, Katherine, Bianca, Gremio, and Hortensio enter. Lucentio and Tranio stand by]

BAPTISTA: Gentlemen, do not beg me any more, for I am firmly resolved not to let my youngest daughter marry before I have a husband for the elder daughter. If either of you love Katherine, because I know you well and love you well, you shall have my permission to court her at your pleasure.

GREMIO: [Aside] To whip her rather. She's too rough for me. There, there, Hortensio, will you have Katherine as a wife?

KAT: I pray you, sir, is it your will
To make a stale of me amongst these mates?

HOR: Mates, maid! how mean you that? no mates for you,
60   Unless you were of gentler, milder mould.

KAT: I'faith, sir, you shall never need to fear:
Iwis it is not half way to her heart;
But if it were, doubt not her care should be
To comb your noddle with a three-legg'd stool
65   And paint your face and use you like a fool.

HOR: From all such devils, good Lord deliver us!

GRE: And me too, good Lord!

TRA: Hush, master! here's some good pastime toward:
That wench is stark mad or wonderful froward.

70 LUC: But in the other's silence do I see
Maid's mild behavior and sobriety.
Peace, Tranio!

TRA: Well said, master; mum! and gaze your fill.

BAP: Gentlemen, that I may soon make good
75   What I have said, Bianca, get you in:
And let it not displease thee, good Bianca,
For I will love thee ne'er the less, my girl.

KAT: A pretty peat! it is best
Put finger in the eye, an she knew why.

80 BIA: Sister, content you in my discontent.
Sir, to your pleasure humbly I subscribe:
My books and instruments shall be my company,
On them to look and practise by myself.

KATHERINE: *Father, is it your will to make me a laughing stock among your mates?*

HORTENSIO: *Mates, maid! What do you mean by that? No mates for you, unless you were of a gentler, milder mold.*

KATHERINE: *To tell you the truth, sir, you do not need to fear. I assure you marriage is something I never think about. But if it were, there is no doubt that I would knock you on the head with a three-legged stool and paint your face with the blood of your wound so you looked like a fool.*

HORTENSIO: *Good Lord, deliver us from all such devils as she!*

GREMIO: *And me too, good Lord!*

TRANIO: *Hush, master! Something great is going to happen here. That wench is stark mad or wonderfully willful.*

LUCENTIO: *But in the other sister's silence I see a maid's mild behavior and sobriety. Be quiet, Tranio!*

TRANIO: *Well said, master; mum's the word! Look at her all you want.*

BAPTISTA: *Gentlemen, I truly mean what I have said. Bianca, go inside; and don't be upset, Bianca, for I love you nevertheless, my dear.*

KATHERINE: *A pretty pet you are! It's best for you to put a finger in your eye and cry, and you know why.*

BIANCA: *Sister, be content in my unhappiness. Father, I humbly submit myself to your will. I will look at my books and practice by myself on my instruments, and they will be my company.*

LUC: Hark, Tranio! thou may'st hear Minerva speak.

85   HOR: Signior Baptista, will you be so strange?
        Sorry am I that our good will effects
        Bianca's grief.

    GRE: Why will you mew her up,
        Signior Baptista, for this fiend of hell,
90   And make her bear the penance of her tongue?

    BAP: Gentlemen, content ye; I am resolved:
        Go in, Bianca: *[Exit Bianca]*
        And for I know she taketh most delight
        In music, instruments and poetry,
95   Schoolmasters will I keep within my house,
        Fit to instruct her youth. If you, Hortensio,
        Or Signior Gremio, you, know any such,
        Prefer them hither; for to cunning men
        I will be very kind, and liberal
100   To mine own children in good bringing up.
        And so farewell. Katherine, you may stay;
        For I have more to commune with Bianca.   *[Exit]*

    KAT: Why, and I trust I may go too, may I not?
        What, shall I be appointed hours; as though, belike, I knew
105   not what to take and what to leave, ha?   *[Exit]*

    GRE: You may go to the devil's dam: your gifts are so good, here's
        none will hold you. Their love is not so great, Hortensio, but
        we may blow our nails together, and fast it fairly out: our
        cake's dough on both sides. Farewell: yet for the love I bear
110   my sweet Bianca, if I can by any means light on a fit man to
        teach her that wherein she delights, I will wish him to her
        father.

    HOR: So will I, Signior Gremio: but a word, I pray. Though the
        nature of our quarrel yet never brooked parle, know now,
115   upon advice, it toucheth us both, that we may yet again have

LUCENTIO: *Listen, Tranio! You can hear Minerva speak.*

HORTENSIO: *Signior Baptista, why will you act so strange? I am sorry that our good will makes Bianca sad.*

GREMIO: *Why will you keep Bianca from our sight, Signior Baptista, for this fiend of hell,* [He points to Katherine] *and make Bianca bear the penance of Katherine's tongue?*

BAPTISTA: *Gentlemen, be content; I am resolved. Go in, Bianca.*
[Bianca exits]
And because I know she takes the most delight in music, instruments, and poetry, I will keep schoolteachers within my house that are fit to instruct her youth. If you, Hortensio, or you, Signior Gremio, know of any instructors, tell them to come here. I will be very kind to cunning men, and I will be liberal to my own children and bring them up well. And so, farewell. Katherine, you may stay; I have more to talk about with Bianca.
[Baptista exits]

KATHERINE: *I believe I can go, too, can't I? What, should I have hours appointed to me, as though I didn't know when to come and when to go? Ha?*
[Katherine exits]

GREMIO: *You may go to the devil's mother! You are so mean and nasty no one will touch you. Woman's love is not so long-lasting, Hortensio; we'll be waiting a long time for this to blow over. We're like a cake that hasn't risen in the oven, dough on both sides. Good-bye. Yet, because I love my sweet Bianca, if I can by any means find a fit man to teach her those things that she delights in, I will bring him to her father.*

HORTENSIO: *So will I, Signior Gremio. But a word with you before you go. Even though our quarrel over Bianca has never come to negotiations, if*

access to our fair mistress and be happy rivals in Bianca's
love, to labour and effect one thing specially.

GRE: What's that, I pray?

HOR: Marry, sir, to get a husband for her sister.

120 GRE: A husband! a devil.

HOR: I say, a husband.

GRE: I say, a devil. Thinkest thou, Hortensio, though her father
be very rich, any man is so very a fool to be married to hell?

HOR: Tush, Gremio, though it pass your patience and mine to
125 endure her loud alarums, why, man, there be good fellows in
the world, an a man could light on them, would take her with
all faults, and money enough.

GRE: I cannot tell; but I had as lief take her dowry with this condition, to be whipped at the high cross every morning.

130 HOR: Faith, as you say, there's small choice in rotten apples. But
come; since this bar in law makes us friends, it shall be so far
forth friendly maintained till by helping Baptista's eldest
daughter to a husband we set his youngest free for a husband,
and then have to't afresh. Sweet Bianca! Happy man be his
135 dole! He that runs fastest gets the ring. How say you, Signior
Gremio?

GRE: I am agreed; and would I had given him the best horse in
Padua to begin his wooing that would thoroughly woo her,
wed her and bed her and rid the house of her! Come on.
[Exeunt Gremio and Hortensio]

140 TRA: I pray, sir, tell me, is it possible
That love should of a sudden take such hold?

36

we work together on one thing, we may yet again have access to our fair mistress and be happy rivals in Bianca's love.

GREMIO: What's that? Please tell me.

HORTENSIO: In truth, sir, to get a husband for her sister.

GREMIO: A husband! A devil.

HORTENSIO: I say, a husband.

GREMIO: I say, a devil. Do you think, Hortensio, although her father is very rich, any man is such a fool as to be married to hell?

HORTENSIO: Nonsense, Gremio. Even though it surpasses your patience and mine to endure her loud, alarm-like screaming, why, man, there are good fellows in the world, if a man could find them, that would take her with all her faults, if the money were high enough.

GREMIO: I'm not so sure of that; if it were me, I'd rather take her dowry and be whipped on the high cross every morning than have to marry her.

HORTENSIO: True, there's not much choice in a bag of rotten apples. But come, since Baptista's refusal makes us friends, our friendship will continue until, by helping Baptista's eldest daughter to a husband, we set his youngest daughter free for a husband, and then we can start our quarrel afresh. Sweet Bianca! He that wins her will be a happy man! He that runs the fastest wins the prize. What do you say, Signior Gremio?

GREMIO: I agree; and I wish I could give the best horse in Padua to the man who would woo, wed, bed and rid the house of Katherine! Come on.
                                        [Gremio and Hortensio exit]

TRANIO: Please, sir, tell me; is it possible that love should all of a sudden take such a hold on you?

LUC: O Tranio, till I found it to be true,
  I never thought it possible or likely;
  But see, while idly I stood looking on,
145 I found the effect of love in idleness:
  And now in plainness do confess to thee,
  That art to me as secret and as dear
  As Anna to the queen of Carthage was,
  Tranio, I burn, I pine, I perish, Tranio,
150 If I achieve not this young modest girl.
  Counsel me, Tranio, for I know thou canst;
  Assist me, Tranio, for I know thou wilt.

TRA: Master, it is no time to chide you now;
  Affection is not rated from the heart:
155 If love have touch'd you, nought remains but so, 'Redime te
  captum quam queas minimo.'

LUC: Gramercies, lad, go forward; this contents:
  The rest will comfort, for thy counsel's sound.

TRA: Master, you look'd so longly on the maid,
160 Perhaps you mark'd not what's the pith of all.

LUC: O yes, I saw sweet beauty in her face,
  Such as the daughter of Agenor had,
  That made great Jove to humble him to her hand,
  When with his knees he kiss'd the Cretan strand.

165 TRA: Saw you no more? mark'd you not how her
      sister
  Began to scold and raise up such a storm
  That mortal ears might hardly endure the din?

LUC: Tranio, I saw her coral lips to move
170 And with her breath she did perfume the air:
  Sacred and sweet was all I saw in her.

TRA: Nay, then, 'tis time to stir him from his trance.

38

LUCENTIO: *Oh, Tranio, I never thought it possible or likely until I found it to be true. But look, while I stood here idly looking on, I fell in love during my idleness. And now in plain truth I confess to you (who know my secrets and are as dear to me as Anna was to the Queen of Carthage), Tranio, I burn for her, I long for her, I will die, Tranio, if I cannot get this young modest girl's love. Advise me, Tranio, for I know you can. Help me, Tranio, for I know you will.*

TRANIO: *Signior, it is no time to yell at you now. Affection cannot be scolded from the heart. If love has touched you, nothing remains but this: "Ransom yourself from captivity as cheaply as you can."*

LUCENTIO: *Many thanks, lad; go forward. This makes me content. You will be given a lot of money because of your good counseling.*

TRANIO: *Master, you looked at her for so long, perhaps you didn't notice what the point of it all was.*

LUCENTIO: *Oh, yes, I saw such sweet beauty in her face as Europa had, she that made the great god Jupiter turn into a bull and bow down to her hand when he courted her on the beach in Crete.*

TRANIO: *That's all you saw? Didn't you see how her sister began to scold and raise up such a storm that mortal ears might hardly endure the sound?*

LUCENTIO: *Tranio, I saw her coral-colored lips move, and when she breathed, she perfumed the air. The sacred and the sweet was all I saw in her.*

TRANIO: *No, then, it is time to break him out of his trance. Please, wake-up,*

I pray, awake, sir: if you love the maid,
Bend thoughts and wits to achieve her. Thus it stands:
175   Her eldest sister is so curst and shrewd
That till the father rid his hands of her,
Master, your love must live a maid at home;
And therefore has he closely mew'd her up,
Because she will not be annoy'd with suitors.

180 Luc: Ah, Tranio, what a cruel father's he!
But art thou not advised, he took some care
To get her cunning schoolmasters to instruct her?

Tra: Ay, marry, am I, sir; and now 'tis plotted.

Luc: I have it, Tranio.

185 Tra: Master, for my hand,
Both our inventions meet and jump in one.

Luc: Tell me thine first.

Tra: You will be schoolmaster
And undertake the teaching of the maid:
190   That's your device.

Luc: It is: may it be done?

Tra: Not possible; for who shall bear your part,
And be in Padua here Vincentio's son,
Keep house and ply his book, welcome his friends,
195   Visit his countrymen and banquet them?

Luc: Basta; content thee, for I have it full.
We have not yet been seen in any house,
Nor can we lie distinguish'd by our faces
For man or master; then it follows thus;
200   Thou shalt be master, Tranio, in my stead,
Keep house and port and servants as I should:

sir! If you love the girl, use your thoughts and wits to achieve her. Here's where it stands: her eldest sister is so cantankerous and sharp of tongue that until the father gets rid of her, master, your love must remain like a maid at home, and, therefore, he has closely confined her so that she will not be annoyed with suitors.

LUCENTIO: Ah, Tranio, he is such a cruel father! But didn't you notice? He took some care to get her some cunning schoolteachers to instruct her.

TRANIO: Yes, in truth, sir, I did notice, and now I have a plan.

LUCENTIO: I have one too, Tranio.

TRANIO: Master, I'll bet both of our inventions are the same.

LUCENTIO: Tell me yours first.

TRANIO: You will be a schoolteacher and teach the maid. That's your device.

LUCENTIO: It is. Can it be done?

TRANIO: It's not possible. Who is going to play you, and pretend to be Vincentio's son here in Padua, take care of his house and study, welcome his friends, visit his countrymen, and give them banquets?

LUCENTIO: Enough! Be content, for I have it! Since we have not yet been seen in any house, no one can tell by our faces who is servant or who is master. Then you will be master, Tranio, instead of me. You will keep a house and food and servants like I would. I will be someone else, someone from Florence, a Neapolitan, or a poorer man of Pisa. Our plan is hatched and we will do it. Tranio, get your clothes changed at once. [They exchange

I will some other be, some Florentine,
Some Neapolitan, or meaner man of Pisa.
'Tis hatch'd and shall be so: Tranio, at once
Uncase thee; take my colour'd hat and cloak:

205 When Biondello comes, he waits on thee;
But I will charm him first to keep his tongue.

  TRA: So had you need.
In brief, sir, sith it your pleasure is,
And I am tied to be obedient;

210 For so your father charged me at our parting,
'Be serviceable to my son,' quoth he,
Although I think 'twas in another sense;
I am content to be Lucentio,
Because so well I love Lucentio.

215 LUC: Tranio, be so, because Lucentio loves:
And let me be a slave, to achieve that maid
Whose sudden sight hath thrall'd my wounded eye.
Here comes the rogue.

[Enter Biondello]
Sirrah, where have you been?

220 BIO: Where have I been! Nay, how now! where are you? Master,
has my fellow Tranio stolen your clothes? Or you stolen his?
or both? Pray, what's the news?

  LUC: Sirrah, come hither: 'tis no time to jest,
And therefore frame your manners to the time.

225 Your fellow Tranio here, to save my life,
Puts my apparel and my countenance on,
And I for my escape have put on his;
For in a quarrel since I came ashore
I kill'd a man and fear I was descried:

230 Wait you on him, I charge you, as becomes,
While I make way from hence to save my life:
You understand me?

42

clothes] *Take my coloured hat and cloak. When Biondello comes, he will be your servant; but I will charm him first so he doesn't give us away.*

TRANIO: *It is important that you do. In brief, sir, since it is your pleasure, and I am your obedient servant (that is what your father said when we left. "Be serviceable to my son," he said, although I think he meant something else), I am content to be Lucentio, because I love Lucentio so well.*

LUCENTIO: *Tranio, be me, because I am in love, and let me be a slave, to achieve that maid whose sudden appearance has enthralled me. Here comes the rogue.*

[Biondello enters]
  Knave, where have you been?

BIONDELLO: *Where have I been? No, what's this? Where are you? Master, has Tranio stolen your clothes? Or you stolen his? Or both? Come on, what's the news?*

LUCENTIO: *Knave, come here. This is no time for jokes, so act in a more serious manner. Your fellow servant, Tranio here, to save my life, has put on my clothing and my outward appearance, and I, in order to escape, have put on his. Since I came ashore I killed a man in a quarrel, and I fear I was seen. I order you to be his servant and wait on him like he is your master while I run away from here to save my life. Do you understand me?*

BIO: I, sir! ne'er a whit.

LUC: And not a jot of Tranio in your mouth:
235   Tranio is changed into Lucentio.

BIO: The better for him: would I were so too!

TRA: So could I, faith, boy, to have the next wish after,
     That Lucentio indeed had Baptista's youngest daughter.
     But, sirrah, not for my sake, but your master's, I advise
240   You use your manners discreetly in all kind of companies:
     When I am alone, why, then I am Tranio;
     But in all places else your master Lucentio.

LUC: Tranio, let's go: one thing more rests, that thyself execute,
     to make one among these wooers: if thou ask me why suf-
245   ficeth my reasons are both good and weighty.   *[Exeunt]*

[The presenters above speak]

1ST SER: My lord, you nod; you do not mind the play.

SLY: Yes, by Saint Anne, do I. A good matter, surely: comes there
     any more of it?

PAG: My lord, 'tis but begun.

250 SLY: 'Tis a very excellent piece of work, madam lady: would
     'twere done!

[They sit and mark]

BIONDELLO: *Who me, sir? Not really.*

LUCENTIO: *And do not call him Tranio. Tranio is changed into me, Lucentio.*

BIONDELLO: *The better for him. I wish I was you, too!*

TRANIO: *I wish I could have the next wish I wish for, that Lucentio had Baptista's youngest daughter. But, knave, not for me, but for your master, I advise you to be discreet in all kinds of company. When I am alone, you can call me Tranio; but everywhere else I must be your master Lucentio.*

LUCENTIO: *Tranio, let's go. One more thing remains that you must do. You have to become one of these wooers of Bianca. If you ask me why, let it suffice that my reasons are both good and weighty.* [They exit]

[The scene shifts back to Sly and the Page at the Inn]

FIRST SERVANT: *My lord, you're nodding off. You do not pay attention to the play.*

SLY: *Yes, by Saint Anne, I do. A good matter, surely. Is there any more of it to come?*

PAGE *My lord, it has just begun.*

SLY: *It is a very excellent piece of work, madam lady. I wish it was done!*

[They sit and watch]

Scene 2
Padua. Before Hortensio's house.

[Enter Petruchio and his man Grumio]

PET: Verona, for a while I take my leave,
　　　To see my friends in Padua, but of all
　　　My best beloved and approved friend,
　　　Hortensio; and I trow this is his house.
5　　 Here, sirrah Grumio; knock, I say.

GRU: Knock, sir! whom should I knock? is there man has
　　　rebused your worship?

PET: Villain, I say, knock me here soundly.

10　 GRU: Knock you here, sir! why, sir, what am I, sir, that I should
　　　knock you here, sir?

PET: Villain, I say, knock me at this gate
　　　And rap me well, or I'll knock your knave's pate.

GRU: My master is grown quarrelsome. I should knock you first,
15　　 and then I know after who comes by the worst.

PET: Will it not be?
　　　Faith, sirrah, an you'll not knock, I'll ring it;
　　　I'll try how you can *sol, fa,* and sing it.
　　　　　　　　　　　　　[He wrings him by the ears.]

GRU: Help, masters, help! my master is mad.

20　 PET: Now, knock when I bid you, sirrah villain!

[Enter Hortensio]

46

SCENE 2
Padua. Before Hortensio's house.

[Enter Petruchio and his servant, Grumio]

PETRUCHIO: *Verona, for a while I leave you to see my friends in Padua, especially my most beloved and proven friend, Hortensio, and I think this is his house. Here, you rogue, Grumio; knock, I say.*

GRUMIO: *Knock, sir! Whom should I knock? Is there a man who has abused your worship?*

PETRUCHIO: *Villain, I say, knock me here as soundly as you can.*

GRUMIO: *Knock you here, sir! Why, sir, what kind of man am I, sir, that I should knock you here, sir?*

PETRUCHIO: *Villain, I say, knock me at this gate and hit well or I'll knock your knavish head.*

GRUMIO: *My master is grown quarrelsome. If I knock you first, then I know who gets the worst of this deal afterwards.*

PETRUCHIO: *It will not be? Fine, rogue, if you'll not knock, I'll ring it. I'll find out how you can sing it.* [He wrings him by the ears]

GRUMIO: *Help, masters, help! My master is mad.*

PETRUCHIO: *Now, knock when I tell you, knavish villain!*

[Enter Hortensio]

HOR: How now! what's the matter? My old friend
    Grumio! and my good friend Petruchio! How do you all at
    Verona?

PET: Signior Hortensio, come you to part the fray?
25   'Con tutto il cuore, ben trovato,' may I say.

HOR: 'Alla nostra casa ben venuto, molto honorato signor mio
    Petruchio.' Rise, Grumio, rise: we will compound this quarrel.

GRU: Nay, 'tis no matter, sir, what he 'leges in Latin. If this be not
    a lawful case for me to leave his service, look you, sir, he bid
30   me knock him and rap him soundly, sir: well, was it fit for a
    servant to use his master so, being perhaps, for aught I see,
    two and thirty, a pip out? Whom would to God I had well
    knock'd at first, then had not Grumio come by the worst.

PET: A senseless villain! Good Hortensio,
35   I bade the rascal knock upon your gate
    And could not get him for my heart to do it.

GRU: Knock at the gate! O heavens! Spake you not these words
    plain, 'Sirrah, knock me here, rap me here, knock me well,
    and knock me soundly'? And come you now with, 'knocking
40   at the gate'?

PET: Sirrah, be gone, or talk not, I advise you.

HOR: Petruchio, patience; I am Grumio's pledge:
    Why, this's a heavy chance 'twixt him and you,
    Your ancient, trusty, pleasant servant, Grumio.
45   And tell me now, sweet friend, what happy gale
    Blows you to Padua here from old Verona?

PET: Such wind as scatters young men through the world,
    To seek their fortunes farther than at home
    Where small experience grows. But in a few,

HORTENSIO: What's this? What's the matter? My old friend Grumio and my good friend Petruchio! How is everyone in Verona?

PETRUCHIO: Signior Hortensio, did you come to break up our fight? "Con tutto il cuore, ben trovato," or "with all my heart, well met," may I say.

HORTENSIO: "Alla nostra casa ben venuto, molto honorato signor mio Petruchio," or "Welcome to our house, my much honored Signior Petruchio." Rise, Grumio, rise. We will settle this quarrel.

GRUMIO: No, it is no matter, sir, what he alleges in Latin. This is a lawful case for me to leave his service! Look you, sir; he asked me to knock him and rap him soundly, sir. Well, was it fit for a servant to use his master in this way, being perhaps, for all I can see, not quite right in the head? Would to God I had well knocked him at first, then I would not have come by the worst.

PETRUCHIO: A senseless villain! Good Hortensio, I asked the rascal to knock upon your gate, and could not get him to do it, for all my effort.

GRUMIO: Knock at the gate! Oh, heavens! Did you not plainly say these words, 'Rogue, knock me here, rap me here, knock me well, and knock me soundly'? And now you come out with, 'knocking at the gate'?

PETRUCHIO: Rogue, be gone, or don't talk, I warn you.

HORTENSIO: Petruchio, patience. I stand by Grumio. Why, this is a grave misfortune between him and you, your long-time, trusty, pleasant servant, Grumio. And tell me now, sweet friend, what happy gale blows you here to Padua from old Verona?

PETRUCHIO: A wind that scatters young men through the world to seek their fortunes farther than they can at home, where only small experience grows. But, in a few words, Signior Hortensio, this is how things are with

50   Signior Hortensio, thus it stands with me:
        Antonio, my father, is deceased;
        And I have thrust myself into this maze,
        Haply to wive and thrive as best I may:
        Crowns in my purse I have and goods at home,
55   And so am come abroad to see the world.

    HOR: Petruchio, shall I then come roundly to thee
        And wish thee to a shrewd ill-favour'd wife?
        Thou'ldst thank me but a little for my counsel:
        And yet I'll promise thee she shall be rich
60   And very rich: but thou'rt too much my friend,
        And I'll not wish thee to her.

    PET: Signior Hortensio, 'twixt such friends as we
        Few words suffice; and therefore, if thou know
        One rich enough to be Petruchio's wife,
65   As wealth is burden of my wooing dance,
        Be she as foul as was Florentius' love,
        As old as Sibyl and as curst and shrewd
        As Socrates' Xanthippe, or a worse,
        She moves me not, or not removes, at least,
70   Affection's edge in me, were she as rough
        As are the swelling Adriatic seas:
        I come to wive it wealthily in Padua;
        If wealthily, then happily in Padua.

    GRU: Nay, look you, sir, he tells you flatly what his mind is: why,
75   give him gold enough and marry him to a puppet or an aglet-
        baby; or an old trot with ne'er a tooth in her head, though she
        have as many diseases as two and fifty horses: why, nothing
        comes amiss, so money comes withal.

    HOR: Petruchio, since we are stepp'd thus far in,
80   I will continue that I broach'd in jest.
        I can, Petruchio, help thee to a wife
        With wealth enough and young and beauteous,
        Brought up as best becomes a gentlewoman:

50

me: Antonio, my father, is deceased and I have thrust myself into this maze, to happily wive and thrive as best I may. I have money in my purse and goods at home, and so I have come abroad to see the world.

HORTENSIO: Petruchio, should I be straight with you and wish a shrewish, bad-tempered wife for you? You wouldn't thank me very much for my counsel. Yet, I'll promise you she will be rich, very rich. But you are too good of a friend, and I'll not wish her on you.

PETRUCHIO: Signior Hortensio, between such friends as we are a few words are enough; therefore, if you know one who is rich enough to be Petruchio's wife (since wealth is the main reason for my wooing dance), if she is as foul as the old hag of Florentius, as old as Sibyl and as bad-tempered as the wife of Socrates, or worse, she would not bother me, or does not remove, at least, affection's edge in me, were she as rough as are the swelling Adriatic seas. I come to take a wealthy wife in Padua; if wealthy, then happily in Padua.

GRUMIO: [To Hortensio] No, pay attention, sir; he tells you exactly what his mind is. Just give him enough gold, and he'll marry a puppet or a spangled doll, or an old hag with not a tooth in her head, even though she has as many diseases as fifty-two horses. Why, he sees nothing wrong, so long as money comes out of it.

HORTENSIO: Petruchio, since we are stepped this far in, I will continue what I brought up as a joke. I can, Petruchio, help you to a wife, who is wealthy enough and young and beauteous, brought up in the best way a gentlewoman can be. Her only fault, and that is fault enough, is that she is intolerably bad-tempered and shrewish and forward, so much beyond

Her only fault, and that is faults enough,
85   Is that she is intolerable curst
And shrewd and froward, so beyond all measure
That, were my state far worser than it is,
I would not wed her for a mine of gold.

PET: Hortensio, peace! thou know'st not gold's effect:
90   Tell me her father's name and 'tis enough;
For I will board her, though she chide as loud
As thunder when the clouds in autumn crack.

HOR: Her father is Baptista Minola,
An affable and courteous gentleman:
95   Her name is Katherine Minola,
Renown'd in Padua for her scolding tongue.

PET: I know her father, though I know not her;
And he knew my deceased father well.
I will not sleep, Hortensio, till I see her;
100   And therefore let me be thus bold with you
To give you over at this first encounter,
Unless you will accompany me thither.

GRU: I pray you, sir, let him go while the humour lasts. O' my
word, an she knew him as well as I do, she would think
105   scolding would do little good upon him: she may perhaps call
him half a score knaves or so: why, that's nothing; an he begin
once, he'll rail in his rope-tricks. I'll tell you what sir, an she
stand him but a little, he will throw a figure in her face and
so disfigure her with it that she shall have no more eyes to
110   see withal than a cat. You know him not, sir.

HOR: Tarry, Petruchio, I must go with thee,
For in Baptista's keep my treasure is:
He hath the jewel of my life in hold,
His youngest daughter, beautiful Bianca,
115   And her withholds from me and other more,
Suitors to her and rivals in my love,
Supposing it a thing impossible,

all measure that, if my financial condition was far worse than it is, I would not wed her for a mine of gold.

PETRUCHIO: Hortensio, quiet! You do not know gold's effect. Tell me her father's name and it is enough; I will wed her, though she yell as loud as thunder when the clouds crack in autumn.

HORTENSIO: Her father is Baptista Minola, an affable and courteous gentleman. Her name is Katherine Minola, renowned in Padua for her scolding tongue.

PETRUCHIO: I know her father, though I don't know her; and he knew my deceased father well. I will not sleep, Hortensio, until I see her; and, therefore, let me be this bold with you. I will leave you here, unless you will accompany me there.

GRUMIO: I plead with you, sir, let him go while this feeling lasts. On my word, if she knew Petruchio as well as I do, she would think scolding would do little good. She may, perhaps, call him knave a half a dozen times or so. Why, that's nothing! If he begins to yell once, he'll use such abusive language with her that he'll be hanged for it. I'll tell you what, sir; if she stands up to him just a little, he will throw a figure of speech in her face and so disfigure her with it that she will be cross-eyed like a cat. You don't know him, sir.

HORTENSIO: Stay a while, Petruchio; I must go with you, for my treasure is in Baptista's castle. He has the jewel of my life in hold: his youngest daughter, beautiful Bianca. He withholds her from me and other suitors, the rivals in my love, and believes it impossible that Katherine will be ever wooed because of those defects I have already told you about. Therefore, Baptista has given this order: none shall have access to Bianca until Katherine the cursed has gotten a husband.

For those defects I have before rehearsed,
That ever Katherine will be woo'd;
120   Therefore this order hath Baptista ta'en,
That none shall have access unto Bianca
Till Katherine the curst have got a husband.

GRU: Katherine the curst!
A title for a maid of all titles the worst.

125 HOR: Now shall my friend Petruchio do me grace,
And offer me disguised in sober robes
To old Baptista as a schoolmaster
Well seen in music, to instruct Bianca;
That so I may, by this device, at least
130   Have leave and leisure to make love to her
And unsuspected court her by herself.

GRU: Here's no knavery! See, to beguile the old folks, how the
young folks lay their heads together!

[Enter Gremio and Lucentio, disguised as Cambio]
Master, master, look about you: who goes there, ha?

135 HOR: Peace, Grumio! it is the rival of my love.
Petruchio, stand by a while.

GRU: A proper stripling and an amorous!

GRE: O, very well; I have perused the note.
Hark you, sir: I'll have them very fairly bound:
140   All books of love, see that at any hand;
And see you read no other lectures to her:
You understand me: over and beside
Signior Baptista's liberality,
I'll mend it with a largess. Take your paper too,
145   And let me have them very well perfumed
For she is sweeter than perfume itself
To whom they go to. What will you read to her?

54

GRUMIO: Katherine the cursed! Of all the titles for a maid, that one's the worst.

HORTENSIO: Now my friend Petruchio will do me a favor, and offer me, disguised in sober robes, to old Baptista as a schoolteacher, talented in music, to instruct Bianca, so I may, by this means, at least have permission and the time to let her know I love her and, unsuspected, court her by herself.

GRUMIO: Here's no trickery! See, how the young folks put their heads together to fool the old folks!

[Enter Gremio: and Lucentio, disguised as Cambio]
Master, master, look behind you. Who is that?

HORTENSIO: Be quiet, Grumio! It is the rival of my love. Petruchio, watch a while.

GRUMIO: [Speaking about old Gremio] Now that's what I call a handsome young man in love!

GREMIO: [To Lucentio, who is disguised as Cambio] Oh, very well, I have looked at the bill. Listen, sir, I'll have them very beautifully bound; they are all books of love. Make sure you see to that no matter what, and see you read no other lectures to her. You understand me. Above and besides Signior Baptista's liberality with money, I'll increase it with a larger sum. Take the papers too, and let me have them very well perfumed, for she to whom they go is sweeter than perfume itself. What will you read to her?

LUC: Whate'er I read to her, I'll plead for you
    As for my patron, stand you so assured,
150   As firmly as yourself were still in place:
    Yea, and perhaps with more successful words
    Than you, unless you were a scholar, sir.

GRE: O this learning, what a thing it is!

GRU: O this woodcock, what an ass it is!

155 PET: Peace, sirrah!

HOR: Grumio, mum! God save you, Signior Gremio.

GRE: And you are well met, Signior Hortensio.
    Trow you whither I am going? To Baptista Minola.
    I promised to inquire carefully
160   About a schoolmaster for the fair Bianca:
    And by good fortune I have lighted well
    On this young man, for learning and behavior
    Fit for her turn, well read in poetry
    And other books, good ones, I warrant ye.

165 HOR: 'Tis well; and I have met a gentleman
    Hath promised me to help me to another,
    A fine musician to instruct our mistress;
    So shall I no whit be behind in duty
    To fair Bianca, so beloved of me.

170 GRE: Beloved of me; and that my deeds shall prove.

GRU: And that his bags shall prove.

HOR: Gremio, 'tis now no time to vent our love:
    Listen to me, and if you speak me fair,
    I'll tell you news indifferent good for either.
175   Here is a gentleman whom by chance I met,
    Upon agreement from us to his liking,

LUCENTIO: *Whatever I read to her, I'll plead with her for you as my patron, rest assured, as firmly as if you yourself were in that place, and perhaps I'll use more successful words than you, unless you were a scholar, sir.*

GREMIO: *Oh, this learning, what a thing it is!*

GRUMIO: *Oh, this old bird, how easily fooled he is!*

PETRUCHIO: *Be quiet, knave!*

HORTENSIO: *Grumio, hush! God save you, Signior Gremio.*

GREMIO: *Welcome, Signior Hortensio. Do you know where I am going? To Baptista Minola. I promised to inquire carefully about a schoolteacher for the fair Bianca. And by good fortune I have discovered this young man, who in learning and behavior is fit for her. He's well read in poetry and other books, good ones, I can guarantee.*

HORTENSIO: *That's great! And I have met a gentleman who has promised to help me find a fine musician to instruct our mistress; so I will not be behind in duty to fair Bianca, who I love so much.*

GREMIO: *Who I love so much, and my deeds shall prove that.*

GRUMIO: *And that his money-bags shall prove.*

HORTENSIO: *Gremio, now is no time to express our love. Listen to me, and if you speak fairly to me, I'll tell you news that is good for both of us. Here is a gentleman whom I met by chance, who, if we agree to the terms he likes, will undertake to woo cursed Katherine, and to marry her, if her dowry pleases him.*

Will undertake to woo curst Katherine,
Yea, and to marry her, if her dowry please.

GRE: So said, so done, is well.
180   Hortensio, have you told him all her faults?

PET: I know she is an irksome brawling scold:
       If that be all, masters, I hear no harm.

GRE: No, say'st me so, friend? What countryman?

PET: Born in Verona, old Antonio's son:
185   My father dead, my fortune lives for me;
       And I do hope good days and long to see.

GRE: O sir, such a life, with such a wife, were strange!
       But if you have a stomach, to't i' God's name:
       You shall have me assisting you in all.
190   But will you woo this wild-cat?

PET: Will I live?

GRU: Will he woo her? ay, or I'll hang her.

PET: Why came I hither but to that intent?
       Think you a little din can daunt mine ears?
195   Have I not in my time heard lions roar?
       Have I not heard the sea puff'd up with winds
       Rage like an angry boar chafed with sweat?
       Have I not heard great ordnance in the field,
       And heaven's artillery thunder in the skies?
200   Have I not in a pitched battle heard
       Loud 'larums, neighing steeds, and trumpets' clang?
       And do you tell me of a woman's tongue,
       That gives not half so great a blow to hear
       As will a chestnut in a farmer's fire?
205   Tush, tush! fear boys with bugs.

58

GREMIO: If his deeds match his words, that is wonderful! Hortensio, have you told him all her faults?

PETRUCHIO: I know she is an irksome, brawling scold. If that is all, masters, I hear no harm in it.

GREMIO: No? Is that so, friend? What country do you come from?

PETRUCHIO: Born in Verona, I am old Antonio's son. My father is dead, my fortune is still alive, and I do hope to see good days for a long time.

GREMIO: Sir, such a life, with such a wife, is strange! But if you have the stomach for it, go ahead. In God's name, you shall have me assisting you in everything. But will you woo this wild cat?

PETRUCHIO: Will I live?

GRUMIO: Will he woo her? Yes, or I'll hang her.

PETRUCHIO: Why did I come here except for that intent? Do you think a little din can daunt my ears? Have I not in my time heard lions roar? Have I not heard the sea, puffed up with winds, rage like an angry boar covered with sweat? Have I not heard great cannons in the field, and heaven's artillery thunder in the skies? Have I not, in a terrible battle, heard loud alarms, neighing steeds, and trumpets clang? And you tell me of a woman's tongue, that does not give half so great a blow to hear as a chestnut popping in a farmer's fire does? Tush, tush! You might as well frighten little boys with monsters.

GRU: For he fears none.

GRE: Hortensio, hark:
    This gentleman is happily arrived,
    My mind presumes, for his own good and ours.

210 HOR: I promised we would be contributors
    And bear his charge of wooing, whatsoe'er.

GRE: And so we will, provided that he win her.

GRU: I would I were as sure of a good dinner.

[Enter Tranio brave, and Biondello]

TRA: Gentlemen, God save you. If I may be bold,
215   Tell me, I beseech you, which is the readiest way
    To the house of Signior Baptista Minola?

BIO: He that has the two fair daughters: is't he you mean?

TRA: Even he, Biondello.

GRE: Hark you, sir; you mean not her to—

220 TRA: Perhaps, him and her, sir: what have you to do?

PET: Not her that chides, sir, at any hand, I pray.

TRA: I love no chiders, sir. Biondello, let's away.

LUC: Well begun, Tranio.

HOR: Sir, a word ere you go;
225   Are you a suitor to the maid you talk of, yea or no?

TRA: And if I be, sir, is it any offence?

GRUMIO: For he fears none.

GREMIO: Hortensio, listen: this gentleman has happily arrived, my mind presumes, for his own good and ours.

HORTENSIO: I promised we would give him money to cover the expense of wooing, whatever it may cost.

GREMIO: And so we will, provided that he win her.

GRUMIO: I wish I were as sure of getting a good dinner.

[Enter Tranio, boldly dressed, and Biondello]

TRANIO: Gentlemen, God save you.   If I may be bold, tell me, I beseech you, which is the fastest way to the house of Signior Baptista Minola?

BIONDELLO: He who has the two fair daughters; is it he you mean?

TRANIO: Yes, he, Biondello.

GREMIO: Excuse me, sir. You don't mean her...

TRANIO: Perhaps, him and her, sir. Why do you care?

PETRUCHIO: Not her who scolds, sir, at any rate, I hope.

TRANIO: I love no chiders, sir. Biondello, let's leave.

LUCENTIO: Well begun, Tranio.

HORTENSIO: Sir, a word with you before you go; are you a suitor to the maid you talk of, yes or no?

TRANIO: And if I am, sir, is it any offense?

GRE: No; if without more words you will get you hence.

TRA: Why, sir, I pray, are not the streets as free
    For me as for you?

230 GRE: But so is not she.

TRA: For what reason, I beseech you?

GRE: For this reason, if you'll know,
    That she's the choice love of Signior Gremio.

HOR: That she's the chosen of Signior Hortensio.

235 TRA: Softly, my masters! if you be gentlemen,
    Do me this right; hear me with patience.
    Baptista is a noble gentleman,
    To whom my father is not all unknown;
    And were his daughter fairer than she is,
240   She may more suitors have and me for one.
    Fair Leda's daughter had a thousand wooers;
    Then well one more may fair Bianca have:
    And so she shall; Lucentio shall make one,
    Though Paris came in hope to speed alone.

245 GRE: What! this gentleman will out-talk us all.

LUC: Sir, give him head: I know he'll prove a jade.

PET: Hortensio, to what end are all these words?

HOR: Sir, let me be so bold as ask you,
    Did you yet ever see Baptista's daughter?

250 TRA: No, sir; but hear I do that he hath two,
    The one as famous for a scolding tongue
    As is the other for beauteous modesty.

GREMIO: *No, if you will get out of here without saying anything else.*

TRANIO: *Why, sir, I ask you, are the streets not as free for me as for you?*

GREMIO: *But she is not.*

TRANIO: *For what reason, I beseech you?*

GREMIO: *For this reason, if you need to know: she's the choice love of Signior Gremio.*

HORTENSIO: *She's the chosen one of Signior Hortensio.*

TRANIO: *Quietly, my masters! If you are gentlemen, do this for me; hear me with patience. Baptista is a noble gentleman, and my father knows him, and if his daughter were less fair than she is, she might have more suitors, and I might be one. Helen of Troy had a thousand wooers; fair Bianca may have one more and so she will. I, Lucentio, will be one, even though Paris himself came in hope to succeed with her.*

GREMIO: *What! This gentleman will out-talk us all.*

LUCENTIO: *Sir, give him room to speak; I know he'll prove a worthless suitor.*

PETRUCHIO: *Hortensio, to what end are all these words?*

HORTENSIO: *Sir, let me be so bold as to ask if you have ever seen Baptista's daughter?*

TRANIO: *No, sir; but I've heard that he has two. One is as famous for a scolding tongue as the other is for beauteous modesty.*

PET: Sir, sir, the first's for me; let her go by.

GRE: Yea, leave that labour to great Hercules;
255   And let it be more than Alcides' twelve.

PET: Sir, understand you this of me in sooth:
          The youngest daughter whom you hearken for
          Her father keeps from all access of suitors,
          And will not promise her to any man
260   Until the elder sister first be wed:
          The younger then is free and not before.

TRA: If it be so, sir, that you are the man
          Must stead us all and me amongst the rest,
          And if you break the ice and do this feat,
265   Achieve the elder, set the younger free
          For our access, whose hap shall be to have her
          Will not so graceless be to be ingrate.

HOR: Sir, you say well and well you do conceive;
          And since you do profess to be a suitor,
270   You must, as we do, gratify this gentleman,
          To whom we all rest generally beholding.

TRA: Sir, I shall not be slack: in sign whereof,
          Please ye we may contrive this afternoon,
          And quaff carouses to our mistress' health,
275   And do as adversaries do in law,
          Strive mightily, but eat and drink as friends.

GRU, BIO: O excellent motion! Fellows, let's be gone.

HOR: The motion's good indeed and be it so,
          Petruchio, I shall be your ben venuto.

                                                    [Exeunt]

PETRUCHIO: *Sir, sir, the first's for me; let her alone.*

GREMIO: [Indicating Petruchio] *Yes, leave that labor to great Hercules; it'll be harder to achieve than the other twelve.*

PETRUCHIO: *Sir, in truth you must understand this: her father keeps the youngest daughter, whom you ask for, from suitors and will not promise her to any man until the elder sister is wed first. The younger is then free, but not before.*

TRANIO: *If it be so, sir, that you are the man who must help us all (and me among the rest), and if you break the ice and do this feat, achieve the elder sister and set the younger free for our access, the man whose happiness it is to have her will not be so graceless as to be an ingrate.*

HORTENSIO: *Sir, you speak well and you understand well. Since you profess to be a suitor, you must, as we do, pay this gentleman, to whom we owe a great deal.*

TRANIO: *Sir, I will not be slack in payment. As proof, therefore, if it pleases you, let's get together this afternoon and drink toasts to our mistress' health, and we'll be like opposing lawyers, who strive mightily in the courtroom, but eat and drink as friends.*

GRUMIO BIONDELLO: *Oh, excellent idea! Fellows, let's go now.*

HORTENSIO: *The idea's good indeed and because it is, Petruchio, I will introduce you, come, let's go!*

[All exit]

❦

65

ACT II

SCENE 1
Padua. A room in Baptista's house.

[Enter Katherine and Bianca]

   BIA: Good sister, wrong me not, nor wrong yourself,
      To make a bondmaid and a slave of me;
      That I disdain: but for these other gawds,
      Unbind my hands, I'll pull them off myself,
5   Yea, all my raiment, to my petticoat;
      Or what you will command me will I do,
      So well I know my duty to my elders.

   KAT: Of all thy suitors, here I charge thee, tell
      Whom thou lovest best: see thou dissemble not.

10 BIA: Believe me, sister, of all the men alive
      I never yet beheld that special face
      Which I could fancy more than any other.

   KAT: Minion, thou liest. Is't not Hortensio?

   BIA: If you affect him, sister, here I swear
15   I'll plead for you myself, but you shall have him.

   KAT: O then, belike, you fancy riches more:
      You will have Gremio to keep you fair.

   BIA: Is it for him you do envy me so?

ACT II

SCENE 1
Padua. A room in Baptista's house.

[Enter Katherine and Bianca]

BIANCA: *Good sister, do not wrong me or wrong yourself by making a tied-up maid and a slave of me; that I disdain. But for my clothing, unbind my hands, and I'll pull them off myself. Yes, all my clothing, down to my petticoat. Whatever you will command me I will do. I know my duty to my elders well.*

KATHERINE: *Of all your suitors, I command you, tell me whom you love best, and see that you don't lie.*

BIANCA: *Believe me, sister, of all men alive, I have never seen that special face I could fancy more than any other.*

KATHERINE: *Hussy, you lie. Isn't it Hortensio?*

BIANCA: *If you like him, sister, I swear I'll plead for you myself, and you shall have him.*

KATHERINE: *Then, it must be that you fancy riches more. You will have Gremio to keep you in beautiful clothing.*

BIANCA: *Is it for him you envy me? No, then you jest, and now I understand,*

Nay then you jest, and now I well perceive
20   You have but jested with me all this while:
I prithee, sister Kate, untie my hands.

KAT: If that be jest, then all the rest was so.   *[Strikes her]*

[Enter Baptista]

BAP: Why, how now, dame! whence grows this insolence?
Bianca, stand aside. Poor girl! she weeps.
25   Go ply thy needle; meddle not with her.
For shame, thou helding of a devilish spirit,
Why dost thou wrong her that did ne'er wrong thee?
When did she cross thee with a bitter word?

KAT: Her silence flouts me, and I'll be revenged.
[Flies after Bianca]

30   BAP: What, in my sight? Bianca, get thee in.   *[Exit Bianca]*

KAT: What, will you not suffer me? Nay, now I see
She is your treasure, she must have a husband;
I must dance bare-foot on her wedding day
And for your love to her lead apes in hell.
35   Talk not to me: I will go sit and weep
Till I can find occasion of revenge.   *[Exit]*

BAP: Was ever gentleman thus grieved as I?
But who comes here?

*[Enter Gremio, Lucentio in the habit of a mean man; Petruchio, with
Hortensio as a musician; and Tranio, with Biondello bearing a lute and
books]*

GRE: Good morrow, neighbour Baptista.

40   BAP: Good morrow, neighbour Gremio.
God save you, gentlemen!

you have only jested with me all this time. I beg, sister Kate, untie my hands.

KATHERINE: *If that is a jest, then all the rest was too.*   [Kate hits her]

[Enter Baptista]

BAPTISTA: *Why, what's going on here, dame! Where does this insolence come from? Bianca, stand aside. Poor girl, she weeps! Go do some sewing; don't meddle with her. For shame, you beast of a devilish spirit, why do you wrong her who never did wrong to you? When did she anger you with a bitter word?*

KATHERINE: *Her silence mocks me, and I'll have revenge.*
[Kate goes after Bianca]

BAPTISTA: *What, in my sight? Bianca, go inside.*   [Bianca exits]

KATHERINE: *You won't allow me to do that? No, now I see. She is your treasure; she must have a husband. I must dance barefoot on her wedding day and, because of your love to her, I have to lead apes in hell. Don't talk to me. I will go sit and weep until I can find an occasion for revenge.*
[Katherine exits]

BAPTISTA: *Was there ever a gentleman as grieved as I am? But who comes here?*

[Enter Gremio, Lucentio in the clothing of a person of lower class; Petruchio, with Hortensio as a musician, and Tranio, with Biondello bearing a lute and books]

GREMIO: *Good morning, neighbor Baptista.*

BAPTISTA: *Good morning, neighbor Gremio. God save you, gentlemen!*

PET: And you, good sir! Pray, have you not a daughter
      Call'd Katherine, fair and virtuous?

BAP: I have a daughter, sir, called Katherine.

45 GRE: You are too blunt: go to it orderly.

PET: You wrong me, Signior Gremio: give me leave.
       I am a gentleman of Verona, sir,
       That, hearing of her beauty and her wit,
       Her affability and bashful modesty,
50   Her wondrous qualities and mild behavior,
       Am bold to show myself a forward guest
       Within your house, to make mine eye the witness
       Of that report which I so oft have heard.
       And, for an entrance to my entertainment,
55   I do present you with a man of mine,
       [Presenting Hortensio]
       Cunning in music and the mathematics,
       To instruct her fully in those sciences,
       Whereof I know she is not ignorant:
       Accept of him, or else you do me wrong:
60   His name is Licio, born in Mantua.

BAP: You're welcome, sir; and he, for your good sake.
      But for my daughter Katherine, this I know,
      She is not for your turn, the more my grief.

PET: I see you do not mean to part with her,
65   Or else you like not of my company.

BAP: Mistake me not; I speak but as I find.
      Whence are you, sir? what may I call your name?

PET: Petruchio is my name; Antonio's son,
      A man well known throughout all Italy.

70 BAP: I know him well: you are welcome for his sake.

70

PETRUCHIO: And you too, good sir! Tell me, don't you have a daughter called Katherine, fair and virtuous?

BAPTISTA: I have a daughter, sir, called Katherine.

GREMIO: You are too blunt. Go about it the right way.

PETRUCHIO: You insult me, Signior Gremio; give me a chance. I am a gentleman of Verona, sir, who hearing of her beauty and her wit, her affability and bashful modesty, her wondrous qualities and mild behavior, is bold to be an unannounced guest within your house, to witness that report which I have so often heard. And, as the price of admission for this entertainment, I give you my man. [Presenting Hortensio] He is cunning in music and mathematics and can instruct her fully in those sciences, in which I know she is not ignorant. Accept him, or else you insult me. His name is Licio, born in Mantua.

BAPTISTA: You're welcome, sir, and so is he, for your good word. But for my daughter Katherine, this I know: she is not your type, and this fills me with grief.

PETRUCHIO: I see you do not mean to part with her, or else you do not like my company.

BAPTISTA: Don't mistake me. I speak what I see. Where are you from, sir? What may I call you?

PETRUCHIO: Petruchio is my name, Antonio's son, a man well known throughout all Italy.

BAPTISTA: I know him well; you are welcome for his sake.

GRE: Saving your tale, Petruchio, I pray,
  Let us, that are poor petitioners, speak too:
  Backare! you are marvellous forward.

PET: O, pardon me, Signior Gremio; I would fain be doing.

75 GRE: I doubt it not, sir; but you will curse your wooing.
  Neighbour, this is a gift very grateful, I am sure of it. To
  express the like kindness, myself, that have been more kindly
  beholding to you than any, freely give unto you this young
  scholar, *[Presenting Lucentio]* that hath been long studying at
80 Rheims; as cunning in Greek, Latin, and other languages, as
  the other in music and mathematics: his name is Cambio;
  pray, accept his service.

BAP: A thousand thanks, Signior Gremio.
  Welcome, good Cambio. *[To Tranio]*
85 But, gentle sir, methinks you walk like a
  stranger: may I be so bold to know the cause of your coming?

TRA: Pardon me, sir, the boldness is mine own,
  That, being a stranger in this city here,
  Do make myself a suitor to your daughter,
90 Unto Bianca, fair and virtuous.
  Nor is your firm resolve unknown to me,
  In the preferment of the eldest sister.
  This liberty is all that I request,
  That, upon knowledge of my parentage,
95 I may have welcome 'mongst the rest that woo
  And free access and favour as the rest:
  And, toward the education of your daughters,
  I here bestow a simple instrument,
  And this small packet of Greek and Latin books:
100 If you accept them, then their worth is great.

BAP: Lucentio is your name; of whence, I pray?

TRA: Of Pisa, sir; son to Vincentio.

72

GREMIO: *With all respect, Petruchio, I beg of you, let us, who are poor petitioners, speak too. Back off for a while! You are very bold.*

PETRUCHIO: *Oh, pardon me, Signior Gremio, I would not want to do so.*

GREMIO: *I don't doubt it, sir, but you will curse your wooing. Neighbor, this is a gift which you will be very grateful for, I am sure of it. To express a similar kindness myself, who has been more generous to you than any, I freely give you this young scholar,* [Presenting Lucentio disguised as Cambio] *who has been studying a long time at Rheims. He is as cunning in Greek, Latin, and other languages, as the other teacher is in music and mathematics. His name is Cambio. I beg you, accept his service.*

BAPTISTA: *A thousand thanks, Signior Gremio. Welcome, good Cambio.* [To Tranio] *But, gentle sir, I think you are a stranger. May I be so bold as to know why you come here?*

TRANIO: *Pardon me, sir, the boldness is my own, because, being a stranger in this city here, I make myself a suitor to your daughter, Bianca, fair and virtuous. I know of your firm resolve to have the eldest sister married first. This liberty is all that I request: that, when you find out who my parents are, I may be welcome among the rest who court and given as much free access and favor as them. Toward the education of your daughters, I here give a simple instrument, and this small packet of Greek and Latin books. If you accept them, they have great worth.*

BAPTISTA: *Lucentio is your name? Please tell me where you are from.*

TRANIO: *From Pisa, sir; I am the son of Vincentio.*

73

BAP: A mighty man of Pisa; by report
     I know him well: you are very welcome, sir.
105   Take you the lute, and you the set of books;
     You shall go see your pupils presently.
     Holla, within!

     [Enter a Servant]
     Sirrah, lead these gentlemen
     To my daughters; and tell them both,
110   These are their tutors: bid them use them well.
          [Exit Servant, with Lucentio and Hortensio, Biondello
          following]
     We will go walk a little in the orchard,
     And then to dinner. You are passing welcome,
     And so I pray you all to think yourselves.

PET: Signior Baptista, my business asketh haste,
115   And every day I cannot come to woo.
     You knew my father well, and in him me,
     Left solely heir to all his lands and goods,
     Which I have better'd rather than decreased:
     Then tell me, if I get your daughter's love,
120   What dowry shall I have with her to wife?

BAP: After my death the one half of my lands,
     And in possession twenty thousand crowns.

PET: And, for that dowry, I'll assure her of
     Her widowhood, be it that she survive me,
125   In all my lands and leases whatsoever:
     Let specialties be therefore drawn between us,
     That covenants may be kept on either hand.

BAP: Ay, when the special thing is well obtain'd,
     That is, her love; for that is all in all.

130 PET: Why, that is nothing: for I tell you, father,
     I am as peremptory as she proud-minded;

74

BAPTISTA: *A mighty man of Pisa; I know him well. You are very welcome, sir.* [To Hortensio as Licio] *You, take you the lute,* [To Lucentio as Cambio] *and you the set of books. You shall go see your pupils immediately. Hello, anyone inside!* [Enter a Servant] *Servant, lead these gentlemen to my daughters, and tell them both that these are their tutors. Tell them to be nice to them.* [Exit Servant, with Lucentio and Hortensio, Biondello following] *We will go walk a little in the orchard, and then to dinner. You are very welcome, and I ask you all to think of yourselves that way.*

PETRUCHIO: *Signior Baptista, my business needs haste, and every day I cannot come to woo. You knew my father well, and through him, me. I am the only heir to all his lands and goods, which I have made more valuable, rather than less. Tell me, if I get your daughter's love, what dowry shall I have when she is my wife?*

BAPTISTA: *After my death you shall have one half of my lands and twenty thousand crowns.*

PETRUCHIO: *For that dowry, I'll assure her that when she is a widow, if she survives me, she will have all my lands and leases. Let special contracts be written up between us, so that these promises may be kept on both sides.*

BAPTISTA: *Yes, when her love is obtained, for that is the only thing that matters.*

PETRUCHIO: *Why, that is nothing. For I tell you, father, I am as decisive as she is proud-minded. Where two raging fires meet, they consume the*

      And where two raging fires meet together
      They do consume the thing that feeds their fury:
      Though little fire grows great with little wind,
135   Yet extreme gusts will blow out fire and all:
      So I to her and so she yields to me;
      For I am rough and woo not like a babe.

BAP: Well mayst thou woo, and happy be thy speed!
      But be thou arm'd for some unhappy words.

140 PET: Ay, to the proof; as mountains are for winds,
      That shake not, though they blow perpetually.

[Re-enter Hortensio, with his head broke]

BAP: How now, my friend! why dost thou look so pale?

HOR: For fear, I promise you, if I look pale.

BAP: What, will my daughter prove a good musician?

145 HOR: I think she'll sooner prove a soldier.
      Iron may hold with her, but never lutes.

BAP: Why, then thou canst not break her to the lute?

HOR: Why, no; for she hath broke the lute to me.
      I did but tell her she mistook her frets,
150   And bow'd her hand to teach her fingering;
      When, with a most impatient devilish spirit,
      'Frets, call you these?' quoth she; 'I'll fume with them:'
      And, with that word, she struck me on the head,
      And through the instrument my pate made way;
155   And there I stood amazed for a while,
      As on a pillory, looking through the lute;
      While she did call me rascal fiddler
      And twangling Jack; with twenty such vile terms,
      As had she studied to misuse me so.

thing that feeds their fury. Though a little fire grows with little wind, extreme gusts will blow out a fire. That's how I'll be to her, and she will yield to me, for I am rough and don't woo like a baby.

BAPTISTA: May you woo well! Be happy in your progress! But you better be armed for some unhappy words.

PETRUCHIO: Yes, and here's the proof: like mountains for winds, they don't shake, even though the wind blows perpetually.

[Re-enter Hortensio, with his head broken]

BAPTISTA: What's wrong, my friend? Why do you look so pale?

HORTENSIO: Because of fear, I promise you, if I look pale.

BAPTISTA: What, will my daughter prove to be a good musician?

HORTENSIO: I think she'll sooner prove a soldier. She may hold iron, but never lutes.

BAPTISTA: Then you cannot break her to the lute?

HORTENSIO: Why, no; she has broken the lute on me. I only told her she made a mistake with the frets of the lute, and I bowed her hand to teach her the fingering, when, with a most impatient devilish spirit, "You call these frets?" she said, "I'll rage with them!" and, with that word, she struck me on the head, and my head made its way through the instrument, and there I stood amazed for a while, as if I were on a pillory, looking through the lute, while she called me "rascal fiddler" and "twangling Jack," and twenty such vile terms, as if had she studied to abuse me this way.

160 PET: Now, by the world, it is a lusty wench;
          I love her ten times more than e'er I did:
          O, how I long to have some chat with her!

    BAP: Well, go with me and be not so discomfited:
          Proceed in practise with my younger daughter;
165   She's apt to learn and thankful for good turns.
          Signior Petruchio, will you go with us,
          Or shall I send my daughter Kate to you?

    PET: I pray you do.   *[Exeunt all but Petruchio]*
          I will attend her here,
170   And woo her with some spirit when she comes.
          Say that she rail; why then I'll tell her plain
          She sings as sweetly as a nightingale:
          Say that she frown, I'll say she looks as clear
          As morning roses newly wash'd with dew:
175   Say she be mute and will not speak a word;
          Then I'll commend her volubility,
          And say she uttereth piercing eloquence:
          If she do bid me pack, I'll give her thanks,
          As though she bid me stay by her a week:
180   If she deny to wed, I'll crave the day
          When I shall ask the banns and when be married.
          But here she comes; and now, Petruchio, speak.

    [Enter Katherine]
          Good morrow, Kate; for that's your name, I hear.

    KAT: Well have you heard, but something hard of hearing:
185   They call me Katherine that do talk of me.

    PET: You lie, in faith; for you are call'd plain Kate,
          And bonny Kate and sometimes Kate the curst;
          But Kate, the prettiest Kate in Christendom,
          Kate of Kate Hall, my super-dainty Kate,
190   For dainties are all Kates, and therefore, Kate,

78

PETRUCHIO: *Now, by the world, she is a lusty wench. I love her ten times more than I ever did. Oh, how I long to speak with her!*

BAPTISTA: *[To Hortensio] Well, go with me and don't be so discouraged. Proceed in practice with my younger daughter. She's inclined to learn and be thankful for good deeds. Signior Petruchio, will you go with us, or shall I send my daughter Kate to you?*

PETRUCHIO: *I ask you to do that. [Exit all but Petruchio] I will await her here, and woo her with some spirit when she comes. Say that she yells; why then, I'll tell her plain that she sings as sweetly as a nightingale. Say that she frowns, and I'll say she looks as clear as morning roses newly washed with dew. Say she is mute and will not speak a word, then I'll commend her fluency of speech and say she utters piercing eloquence. If she tells me to leave, I'll thank her, as though she asked me to stay by her for a week. If she refuses to wed, I'll ask her for the day when I should announce our wedding in the church and when we will be married. But here she comes—and now, Petruchio, speak.*

[Katherine enters]
Good morning, Kate, for that's your name, I hear.

KATHERINE: *You have heard well, but you're a little hard of hearing. They who talk of me call me Katherine.*

PETRUCHIO: *You lie, I'm sure, for you are simply called Kate, and big, stout Kate, and sometimes, Kate the cursed. But Kate, the prettiest Kate in Christendom, Kate of Kate Hall, my super-dainty Kate, (for dainties are all Kates)—and, therefore, Kate, take this of me, Kate of my consolation: Hearing your mildness praised in every town, your virtues spoken of,*

Take this of me, Kate of my consolation;
Hearing thy mildness praised in every town,
Thy virtues spoke of, and thy beauty sounded,
Yet not so deeply as to thee belongs,
195   Myself am moved to woo thee for my wife.

KAT: Moved! in good time: let him that moved you hither
Remove you hence: I knew you at the first
You were a moveable.

PET: Why, what's a moveable?

200 KAT: A join'd-stool.

PET: Thou hast hit it: come, sit on me.

KAT: Asses are made to bear, and so are you.

PET: Women are made to bear, and so are you.

KAT: No such jade as you, if me you mean.

205 PET: Alas! good Kate, I will not burden thee;
For, knowing thee to be but young and light—

KAT: Too light for such a swain as you to catch;
And yet as heavy as my weight should be.

PET: Should be! should—buzz!

210 KAT: Well ta'en, and like a buzzard.

PET: O slow-wing'd turtle! shall a buzzard take thee?

KAT: Ay, for a turtle, as he takes a buzzard.

215 PET: Come, come, you wasp; i' faith, you are too angry.

and your beauty as well, (but not so deeply as you deserve), I am moved to woo you for my wife.

KATHERINE: *Moved! Indeed, let him that moved you here remove you from here. I knew at first glance that you were a moveable man.*

PETRUCHIO: *Why, what's "moveable"?*

KATHERINE: *A three legged stool.*

PETRUCHIO: *You are right. Come, sit on me.*

KATHERINE: *Asses are made to bear burdens, and so are you.*

PETRUCHIO: *Women are made to bear children, and so are you.*

KATHERINE: *Not from such a worthless horse as you, if you mean me.*

PETRUCHIO: *Alas, good Kate, I will not burden you, for, knowing you to be young and light–*

KATHERINE: *Too light and quick for a dimwit like you to catch; and yet as heavy as my weight should be.*

PETRUCHIO: *Should be! Should buzz...like a bee!*

KATHERINE: *I get it! Also, like a buzzard.*

PETRUCHIO: *Oh, slow-winged turtledove! Would a buzzard take you?*

KATHERINE: *Yes, for a turtle, as he takes after a buzzard.*

PETRUCHIO: *Come, come, you wasp. I swear, you are too angry.*

KAT: If I be waspish, best beware my sting.

PET: My remedy is then, to pluck it out.

KAT: Ay, if the fool could find it where it lies,

220 PET: Who knows not where a wasp does wear his sting? In his
    tail.

KAT: In his tongue.

PET: Whose tongue?

KAT: Yours, if you talk of tails: and so farewell.

PET: What, with my tongue in your tail? nay, come again,
225   Good Kate; I am a gentleman.

KAT: That I'll try.   *[She strikes him]*

PET: I swear I'll cuff you, if you strike again.

KAT: So may you lose your arms:
       If you strike me, you are no gentleman;
230   And if no gentleman, why then no arms.

PET: A herald, Kate? O, put me in thy books!

KAT: What is your crest? a coxcomb?

PET: A combless cock, so Kate will be my hen.

KAT: No cock of mine; you crow too like a craven.

235 PET: Nay, come, Kate, come; you must not look so sour.

KAT: It is my fashion, when I see a crab.

KATHERINE: *If I am waspish, you better beware of my sting.*

PETRUCHIO: *Then my remedy is to pluck it out.*

KATHERINE: *Yes, if the fool could find where it is.*

PETRUCHIO: *Who does not know where a wasp wears his sting? In his tail.*

KATHERINE: *In his tongue.*

PETRUCHIO: *Whose tongue?*

KATHERINE: *Yours, if you talk of tales, and so farewell.*

PETRUCHIO: *What, with my tongue in your tail? No, try again, Good Kate. I am a gentleman.*

KATHERINE: *That I'll try.*   [She strikes him]

PETRUCHIO: *I swear, I'll cuff you if you strike me again.*

KATHERINE: *If you do, may you lose your arms. If you strike me, you are not a gentleman; and if you are no gentleman, why, then, you have no coat of arms.*

PETRUCHIO: *Am I a herald, Kate? Oh, put me in your books!*

KATHERINE: *What is your crest? The comb of a rooster?*

PETRUCHIO: *A combless rooster; therefore, Kate will be my hen.*

KATHERINE: *No rooster of mine. You crow too much like a coward.*

PETRUCHIO: *No, come, Kate, come. You must not look so sour.*

KATHERINE: *It's what I do when I see a crab.*

PET: Why, here's no crab; and therefore look not sour.

KAT: There is, there is.

PET: Then show it me.

240 KAT: Had I a glass, I would.

PET: What, you mean my face?

KAT: Well aim'd of such a young one.

PET: Now, by Saint George, I am too young for you.

KAT: Yet you are wither'd.

245 PET: 'Tis with cares.

KAT: I care not.

PET: Nay, hear you, Kate: in sooth you scape not so.

KAT: I chafe you, if I tarry: let me go.

PET: No, not a whit: I find you passing gentle.
250   'Twas told me you were rough and coy and sullen,
     And now I find report a very liar;
     For thou are pleasant, gamesome, passing courteous,
     But slow in speech, yet sweet as spring-time flowers:
     Thou canst not frown, thou canst not look askance,
255   Nor bite the lip, as angry wenches will,
     Nor hast thou pleasure to be cross in talk,
     But thou with mildness entertain'st thy wooers,
     With gentle conference, soft and affable.
     Why does the world report that Kate doth limp?
260   O slanderous world! Kate like the hazel-twig
     Is straight and slender and as brown in hue
     As hazel nuts and sweeter than the kernels.
     O, let me see thee walk: thou dost not halt.

84

PETRUCHIO: *Why, there's no crab here, and, therefore, don't look sour.*

KATHERINE: *There is, there is.*

PETRUCHIO: *Then show it me.*

KATHERINE: *If I had a mirror, I would.*

PETRUCHIO: *What, you mean my face?*

KATHERINE: *Guessed well by such a child.*

PETRUCHIO: *Now, by Saint George, I am too young for you.*

KATHERINE: *Yet you are withered.*

PETRUCHIO: *Withered with cares.*

KATHERINE: *I don't care.*

PETRUCHIO: *No, listen, Kate—in truth, you can't escape so easily.*

KATHERINE: *I'll annoy you, if I stay. Let me go.*

PETRUCHIO: *No, not a bit. I find you very gentle. It was told to me that you were rough and coy and sullen, and now I find that report a liar. For you are pleasant, playful, very courteous, slow in speech, yet sweet as springtime flowers. You cannot frown, you cannot look scornful, nor bite your lip, as angry wenches will, nor do you take pleasure in angry talk. But you entertain your wooers with mildness, with gentle conversation, soft and cordial. Why does the world report that Kate limps? Oh, slanderous world! Kate, like the hazel-twig, is straight and slender and as brown as hazel nuts and sweeter than the kernels. Let me see you walk; you do not limp.*

KAT: Go, fool, and whom thou keep'st command.

265 PET: Did ever Dian so become a grove
As Kate this chamber with her princely gait?
O, be thou Dian, and let her be Kate;
And then let Kate be chaste and Dian sportful!

KAT: Where did you study all this goodly speech?

270 PET: It is extempore, from my mother-wit.

KAT: A witty mother! witless else her son.

PET: Am I not wise?

KAT: Yes; keep you warm.

PET: Marry, so I mean, sweet Katherine, in thy bed:
275 And therefore, setting all this chat aside,
Thus in plain terms: your father hath consented
That you shall be my wife; your dowry 'greed on;
And, will you, nill you, I will marry you.
Now, Kate, I am a husband for your turn;
280 For, by this light, whereby I see thy beauty,
Thy beauty, that doth make me like thee well,
Thou must be married to no man but me;
For I am he am born to tame you, Kate,
And bring you from a wild Kate to a Kate
285 Conformable as other household Kates.
Here comes your father: never make denial;
I must and will have Katherine to my wife.

[Re-enter Baptista, Gremio, and Tranio]

BAP: Now, Signior Petruchio, how speed you with my daughter?

PET: How but well, sir? how but well?
290 It were impossible I should speed amiss.

KATHERINE: *Go, fool, and command your servants.*

PETRUCHIO: *Did the chaste goddess Diana ever fill a grove with beauty as Kate fills this chamber with her royal steps? You be Dian, and let Dian be Kate, and then let Kate be chaste and Dian lustful!*

KATHERINE: *Where did you prepare all this flattering speech?*

PETRUCHIO: *It is being made up as I go along, from the wit my mother gave me.*

KATHERINE: *A witty mother! Her son is witless.*

PETRUCHIO: *Am I not wise?*

KATHERINE: *Yes, about enough to keep you warm.*

PETRUCHIO: *True, and I mean, sweet Katherine, to keep you in your bed. Therefore, setting all this chat aside, this is it in plain terms: your father has consented for you to be my wife; your dowry is agreed on, and, whether you like it or not, I will marry you. Now, Kate, I am a husband who is just right for you, for, by this light, where I see your beauty, it makes me like you. You must be married to no man but me. For I am the man who was born to tame you, Kate, and bring you from a wild Kate to a conformable Kate as other household Kates are. Here comes your father. Never deny this: I must and will have Katherine as my wife.*

[Re-enter Baptista, Gremio, and Tranio]

BAPTISTA: *Now, Signior Petruchio, how do you succeed with my daughter?*

PETRUCHIO: *How else but well, sir? How else but well? It was impossible that I should not succeed.*

BAP: Why, how now, daughter Katherine! in your dumps?

KAT: Call you me daughter? now, I promise you
You have show'd a tender fatherly regard,
To wish me wed to one half lunatic;
295   A mad-cup ruffian and a swearing Jack,
That thinks with oaths to face the matter out.

PET: Father, 'tis thus: yourself and all the world,
That talk'd of her, have talk'd amiss of her:
If she be curst, it is for policy,
300   For she's not froward, but modest as the dove;
She is not hot, but temperate as the morn;
For patience she will prove a second Grissel,
And Roman Lucrece for her chastity:
And to conclude, we have 'greed so well together,
305   That upon Sunday is the wedding-day.

KAT: I'll see thee hang'd on Sunday first.

GRE: Hark, Petruchio; she says she'll see thee hang'd first.

TRA: Is this your speeding? nay, then, good night our part!

PET: Be patient, gentlemen; I choose her for myself:
310   If she and I be pleased, what's that to you?
'Tis bargain'd 'twixt us twain, being alone,
That she shall still be curst in company.
I tell you, 'tis incredible to believe
How much she loves me: O, the kindest Kate!
315   She hung about my neck; and kiss on kiss
She vied so fast, protesting oath on oath,
That in a twink she won me to her love.
O, you are novices! 'Tis a world to see,
How tame, when men and women are alone,
320   A meacock wretch can make the curstest shrew.
Give me thy hand, Kate: I will unto Venice,
To buy apparel 'gainst the wedding-day.

BAPTISTA: *Why, what's this, daughter Katherine! Down in the dumps?*

KATHERINE: *Do you call me daughter? Now, I assure you that you have showed a tender fatherly regard, to wish me to wed a half-lunatic, a mad-cap ruffian, and a swearing Jack, who thinks he can swear and get his own way.*

PETRUCHIO: *Father, it is like this. Yourself and all the world, who talked about her, have talked wrongly of her. If she is cross, it is for cunning, for she's not bold, but modest as the dove; she is not hot, but temperate as the morning. As for patience, she will turn out to be a second Griselda, and she'll be like the Roman Lucrece in her chastity. To conclude, we have agreed so well together that the wedding-day is Sunday.*

KATHERINE: *I'll see you hanged on Sunday first.*

GREMIO: *Listen to that, Petruchio; she says she'll see you hanged first.*

TRANIO: *Is this your success? Good night to our part in this business.*

PETRUCHIO: *Be patient, gentlemen. I choose her for myself. If she and I are pleased, what's that to you? It is bargained, between the two of us, that she will still be cross in company. I tell you, it is incredible to believe how much she loves me. Oh, the kindest Kate! She hung about my neck, and piled on kisses so fast, giving oath on oath, that in the twinkling of an eye, she won me to her love. Oh, you are novices! It is worth the world to see how tame, when men and women are alone, a weak, little wretch can make the most cursed shrew. Give me your hand, Kate. I will go to Venice, to buy apparel in preparation for the wedding-day. Provide the feast, father, and invite the guests; I will be sure my Katherine will be finely dressed.*

Provide the feast, father, and bid the guests;
I will be sure my Katherine shall be fine.

325 BAP: I know not what to say: but give me your hands;
God send you joy, Petruchio! 'Tis a match.

GRE, TRA: Amen, say we: we will be witnesses.

PET: Father, and wife, and gentlemen, adieu;
I will to Venice; Sunday comes apace:
330 We will have rings and things and fine array;
And kiss me, Kate, we will be married o'Sunday.
[Exeunt Petruchio and Katherine severally]

GRE: Was ever match clapp'd up so suddenly?

BAP: Faith, gentlemen, now I play a merchant's part,
And venture madly on a desperate mart.

335 TRA: 'Twas a commodity lay fretting by you:
'Twill bring you gain, or perish on the seas.

BAP: The gain I seek is quiet in the match.

GRE: No doubt but he hath got a quiet catch.
But now, Baptista, to your younger daughter:
340 Now is the day we long have looked for:
I am your neighbour, and was suitor first.

TRA: And I am one that love Bianca more
Than words can witness, or your thoughts can guess.

GRE: Youngling, thou canst not love so dear as I.

345 TRA: Graybeard, thy love doth freeze.

BAPTISTA: *I don't know what to say, but give me your hands. God send you joy, Petruchio! It is a match.*

GREMIO, TRANIO: *Amen, we say. We will be witnesses.*

PETRUCHIO: *Father, and wife, and gentlemen, adieu. I will go to Venice. Sunday comes quickly. We will have rings and things and fine clothes for our wedding day. Kiss me, Kate. We will be married on Sunday.*
[Petruchio and Katherine exit separately]

GREMIO: *Was a match ever joined so suddenly?*

BAPTISTA: *True, gentlemen, now I play a merchant's part, and take a chance, madly, in a desperate market.*

TRANIO: *She was a commodity that was bothering you. Like merchandise that will bring you gain, or perish on the seas.*

BAPTISTA: *The gain I seek is quiet in the house because Katherine has been matched.*

GREMIO: *No doubt that Petruchio got a quiet catch. But now, Baptista, to your younger daughter. Now is the day we have looked forward to. I am your neighbor, and was her suitor first.*

TRANIO: *I am one that loves Bianca more than words can explain or your thoughts can guess.*

GREMIO: *Youngster, you cannot love as dearly as I can.*

TRANIO: *Graybeard, your love is frozen.*

GRE: But thine doth fry.
Skipper, stand back: 'tis age that nourisheth.

TRA: But youth in ladies' eyes that flourisheth.

BAP: Content you, gentlemen: I will compound this strife:
350   'Tis deeds must win the prize; and he of both
That can assure my daughter greatest dower
Shall have my Bianca's love.
Say, Signior Gremio, What can you assure her?

GRE: First, as you know, my house within the city
355   Is richly furnished with plate and gold;
Basins and ewers to lave her dainty hands;
My hangings all of Tyrian tapestry;
In ivory coffers I have stuff'd my crowns;
In cypress chests my arras counterpoints,
360   Costly apparel, tents, and canopies,
Fine linen, Turkey cushions boss'd with pearl,
Valance of Venice gold in needlework,
Pewter and brass and all things that belong
To house or housekeeping: then, at my farm
365   I have a hundred milch-kine to the pail,
Sixscore fat oxen standing in my stalls,
And all things answerable to this portion.
Myself am struck in years, I must confess;
And if I die to-morrow, this is hers,
370   If whilst I live she will be only mine.

TRA: That 'only' came well in. Sir, list to me:
I am my father's heir and only son:
If I may have your daughter to my wife,
I'll leave her houses three or four as good,
375   Within rich Pisa walls, as any one
Old Signior Gremio has in Padua;
Besides two thousand ducats by the year
Of fruitful land, all which shall be her jointure.
What, have I pinch'd you, Signior Gremio?

GREMIO: *But yours fries. Fellow, stand back; it is age that nourishes.*

TRANIO: *But it is youth in ladies' eyes that flourishes.*

BAPTISTA: *Be calm, gentlemen. I will settle this strife. It is deeds that must win the prize; whichever one of you two can assure my daughter of the greatest amount when he dies shall have my Bianca's love. Signior Gremio, what can you give her?*

GREMIO: *First, as you know, my house within the city is richly furnished with silver plates and gold, with basins and pitchers to wash her dainty hands. My wall-hangings are all of purple tapestry; I have stuffed my gold coins in ivory coffers, and my tapestries in cypress chests. Costly apparel, tents, and canopies, fine linen, Turkish cushions embossed with pearl, Venetian draperies with golden needlework, pewter and brass and all things that belong to a house or housekeeping. Then, at my farm, I have a hundred milk-cows, one hundred and twenty fat oxen standing in my stalls, and all things consistent with my wealth. I, myself, am advanced in years, I must confess, and if I die tomorrow, this is hers if, while I live, she will be only mine.*

TRANIO: *I am glad you said "only." Sir, listen to me: I am my father's heir and only son. If I may have your daughter as my wife, I'll leave her three or four houses within the rich walls of Pisa, as good as any old Signior Gremio has in Padua. In addition, two thousand gold coins per year from fruitful land shall be her inheritance when I die. What, have I pinched you, Signior Gremio?*

380 GRE: Two thousand ducats by the year of land!
    My land amounts not to so much in all:
    That she shall have; besides an argosy
    That now is lying in Marseilles' road.
    What, have I choked you with an argosy?

385 TRA: Gremio, 'tis known my father hath no less
    Than three great argosies; besides two galliases,
    And twelve tight galleys: these I will assure her,
    And twice as much, whate'er thou offer'st next.

    GRE: Nay, I have offer'd all, I have no more;
390   And she can have no more than all I have:
    If you like me, she shall have me and mine.

    TRA: Why, then the maid is mine from all the world,
    By your firm promise: Gremio is out-vied.

    BAP: I must confess your offer is the best;
395   And, let your father make her the assurance,
    She is your own; else, you must pardon me,
    if you should die before him, where's her dower?

    TRA: That's but a cavil: he is old, I young.

    GRE: And may not young men die, as well as old?

400 BAP: Well, gentlemen,
    I am thus resolved: on Sunday next you know
    My daughter Katherine is to be married:
    Now, on the Sunday following, shall Bianca
    Be bride to you, if you make this assurance;
405   If not, Signior Gremio:
    And so, I take my leave, and thank you both.

    GRE: Adieu, good neighbour.   [Exit Baptista]
    Now I fear thee not:
    Sirrah young gamester, your father were a fool

GREMIO: *Two thousand gold coins per year from your land! My land does not amount to that much. She shall have a huge trading ship that now is in the harbor at Marseilles' road. What, have I choked you with a trading ship?*

TRANIO: *Gremio, it is known that my father has no less than three great trading ships, two large galley ships, and twelve watertight galleys. These, I will assure her, and twice as much of whatever you offer next.*

GREMIO: *No, I have offered all. I have no more, and she can have no more than all I have.* [To Baptista] *If you like me, she will have me and everything that's mine.*

TRANIO: *Why, then the maid is mine; all the world knows, your firm promise. Gremio is out-bid.*

BAPTISTA: *I must confess your offer is the best, and, if your father guarantees it, she is your own; otherwise, you must pardon me. If you should die before him, what's her inheritance?*

TRANIO: *That's pointless. He is old; I am young.*

GREMIO: *Don't young men die, as well as old?*

BAPTISTA: *Well, gentlemen, I have resolved it. Next Sunday, you know my daughter Katherine is to be married. On the following Sunday, Bianca will be your bride, if you guarantee this inheritance. If not, she will wed Signior Gremio. And so, I leave and thank you both.*

GREMIO: *Adieu, good neighbor.* [Baptista exits]
Now I don't fear you, knavish young gambler; your father would be a

95

410   To give thee all, and in his waning age
      Set foot under thy table: tut, a toy!
      An old Italian fox is not so kind, my boy.   *[Exit]*

      TRA: A vengeance on your crafty wither'd hide!
             Yet I have faced it with a card of ten.
415   'Tis in my head to do my master good:
             I see no reason but supposed Lucentio
             Must get a father, call'd 'supposed Vincentio;'
             And that's a wonder: fathers commonly
             Do get their children; but in this case of wooing,
420   A child shall get a sire, if I fail not of my cunning
             .

                                                           [Exit]

❧

fool to give you everything, and, in his waning age, be like a guest at your table. Ha, a joke! An old Italian fox is not so generous, my boy.

[Gremio exits]

TRANIO: *I'll have revenge on your crafty, withered hide! I have made a good bluff without a decent card in my deck. It is in my head to do my master good. I see no solution except that supposed Lucentio must get a father called, "supposed Vincentio." That's a wonder. Fathers usually get their children. In this case, a child shall get a father, if I don't fail in my cunning.*

[Tranio exits]

ACT III

Scene 1
Padua. Baptista's house.

[Enter Lucentio, Hortensio, and Bianca]

LUC: Fiddler, forbear; you grow too forward, sir:
    Have you so soon forgot the entertainment
    Her sister Katherine welcomed you withal?

HOR: But, wrangling pedant, this is
5   The patroness of heavenly harmony:
    Then give me leave to have prerogative;
    And when in music we have spent an hour,
    Your lecture shall have leisure for as much.

LUC: Preposterous ass, that never read so far
10   To know the cause why music was ordain'd!
    Was it not to refresh the mind of man
    After his studies or his usual pain?
    Then give me leave to read philosophy,
    And while I pause, serve in your harmony.

15 HOR: Sirrah, I will not bear these braves of thine.

BIA: Why, gentlemen, you do me double wrong,
    To strive for that which resteth in my choice:
    I am no breeching scholar in the schools;
    I'll not be tied to hours nor 'pointed times,
20   But learn my lessons as I please myself.

ACT III

SCENE 1
Padua. Baptista's house.

[Lucentio, Hortensio, and Bianca enter]

LUCENTIO: [as Cambio] *Fiddler, give up. You grow too bold, sir. Have you forgotten the entertainment her sister Katherine welcomed you with so soon?*

HORTENSIO: [as Licio] *Wrangling, pedantic teacher, this is the patroness of heavenly harmony. Give me permission to go first, and when we have spent an hour on music, your lecture will have just as much time.*

LUCENTIO: *Preposterous ass, who never read far enough to know why music was created! Was it not to refresh the mind of man after his studies or his usual pain? Give me permission to read philosophy, and while I pause, present your lessons of harmony.*

HORTENSIO: *Knave, I will not bear these defiant statements of yours.*

BIANCA: *Why, gentlemen, you insult me doubly, to desire that which is my choice. I am no young student, who will be whipped in the schools. I'll not be tied to hours nor appointed times, but learn my lessons to please myself. And, to cut off all argument, let us sit down. [To Hortensio] You*

And, to cut off all strife, here sit we down:
Take you your instrument, play you the whiles;
His lecture will be done ere you have tuned.

HOR: You'll leave his lecture when I am in tune?

25 LUC: That will be never: tune your instrument.

BIA: Where left we last?

LUC: Here, madam:
    'Hic ibat Simois; hic est Sigeia tellus;
    Hic steterat Priami regia celsa senis.'

30 BIA:Construe them.

LUC: 'Hic ibat,' as I told you before,–'Simois,' I am
    Lucentio,–'hic est,' son unto Vincentio of Pisa,–
    'Sigeia tellus,' disguised thus to get your love;–
    'Hic steterat,' and that Lucentio that comes
35   a-wooing,–'Priami,' is my man Tranio,–'regia,'
    bearing my port,–'celsa senis,' that we might
    beguile the old pantaloon.

HOR: Madam, my instrument's in tune.

BIA: Let's hear. O fie! the treble jars.

40 LUC: Spit in the hole, man, and tune again.

BIA: Now let me see if I can construe it: 'Hic ibat
    Simois,' I know you not,–'hic est Sigeia tellus,'
    I trust you not,–'Hic steterat Priami,' take heed
    he hear us not,–'regia,' presume not,–'celsa
45   senis,' despair not.

HOR: Madam, 'tis now in tune.

100

take your instrument and play a while. His lecture will be done before you have tuned.

HORTENSIO: *You'll leave his lecture when I am in tune?*

LUCENTIO: *That will be never. Tune your instrument.*

BIANCA: *Where did we leave off last?*

LUCENTIO: *Here, madam: "Hic ibat Simois; hic est Sigeia tellus; Hic steterat Priami regia celsa senis."*

BIANCA: *Interpret this.*

LUCENTIO: *"Hic ibat" means "as I told you before"; "Simois," "I am Lucentio"; "hic est" is "son of Vincentio of Pisa." "Sigeia tellus" means "disguised like this to get your love." "Hic steterat" is "Lucentio that comes to woo you"; "Priami" is "my servant, Tranio," "regia" means "acting like me," and "celsa senis" is "so that we might fool your father."*

HORTENSIO: *Madam, my instrument's in tune.*

BIANCA: *Let's hear. [He plays] Oh, horrors! The treble notes are out of tune.*

LUCENTIO: *Spit in the hole, man, and tune again.*

BIANCA: *Now let me see if I can understand it: "Hic ibat Simois" is "I don't know you"; "hic est Sigeia tellus" means "I don't trust you"; "Hic steterat Priami" is "be careful that he doesn't hear us," "regia" is "presume not" and "celsa senis" is "do not despair."*

HORTENSIO: *Madam, it is now in tune.*

LUC: All but the bass.

HOR: The base is right; 'tis the base knave that jars.
      [Aside] How fiery and forward our pedant is!
50   Now, for my life, the knave doth court my love:
      Pedascule, I'll watch you better yet.

BIA: In time I may believe, yet I mistrust.

LUC: Mistrust it not: for, sure, Æacides
      Was Ajax, call'd so from his grandfather.

55 BIA: I must believe my master; else, I promise you,
      I should be arguing still upon that doubt:
      But let it rest. Now, Licio, to you:
      Good masters, take it not unkindly, pray,
      That I have been thus pleasant with you both.

60 HOR: You may go walk, and give me leave a while:
      My lessons make no music in three parts.

LUC: Are you so formal, sir? well, I must wait,
      [Aside] And watch withal; for, but I be deceived,
      Our fine musician groweth amorous.

65 HOR: Madam, before you touch the instrument,
      To learn the order of my fingering,
      I must begin with rudiments of art;
      To teach you gamut in a briefer sort,
      More pleasant, pithy and effectual,
70   Than hath been taught by any of my trade:
      And there it is in writing, fairly drawn.

BIA: Why, I am past my gamut long ago.

HOR: Yet read the gamut of Hortensio.

LUCENTIO: *All but the bass notes.*

HORTENSIO: *The bass is right; it is the base knave that is out of tune. How fiery and bold our pedant is! Now, I swear, the knave courts my love. Little schoolmaster, I'll watch you even closer than before.*

BIANCA: *In time I may believe, but now I mistrust.*

LUCENTIO: [Pretending to teach] *Do not mistrust it, for surely, Aeacides was Ajax, named so from his grandfather.*

BIANCA: *I must believe my teacher, or else, I promise you, I should still be arguing. But let it rest. Now, Licio, to you. Good teachers, do not take it unkindly, please, that I have been this pleasant with both of you.*

HORTENSIO: [To Lucentio] *You may go for a walk, and leave me alone for a while. My lessons are not for music in three parts.*

LUCENTIO: *Are you so formal, sir? Well, I must wait.* [Aside] *And watch, too, for, unless I am deceived, our fine musician grows amorous.*

HORTENSIO: *Madam, before you touch the instrument, to learn how to play it with your fingers, I must begin with the basics of art, to teach you the musical scale quickly and more pleasantly, forcefully, and effectively than has been taught by anyone of my trade. And there it is in writing, easily understood.*

BIANCA: *Why, I passed my musical scales long ago.*

HORTENSIO: *Yet read the musical scale of Hortensio.*

103

BIA: *[Reads]*
75   "Gamut' I am, the ground of all accord,
             'A re,' to plead Hortensio's passion;
             'B mi,' Bianca, take him for thy lord,
              'C fa ut,' that loves with all affection:
             'D sol re,' one clef, two notes have I:
80   'E la mi,' show pity, or I die.'
          Call you this gamut? tut, I like it not:
          Old fashions please me best; I am not so nice,
          To change true rules for odd inventions.

          [Enter a Servant]

SER: Mistress, your father prays you leave your books
85   And help to dress your sister's chamber up:
          You know to-morrow is the wedding-day.

BIA: Farewell, sweet masters both; I must be gone.
                              [Exeunt Bianca and Servant]

LUC: Faith, mistress, then I have no cause to stay.   *[Exit]*

HOR: But I have cause to pry into this pedant:
90   Methinks he looks as though he were in love:
          Yet if thy thoughts, Bianca, be so humble
          To cast thy wandering eyes on every stale,
          Seize thee that list: if once I find thee ranging,
          Hortensio will be quit with thee by changing.   *[Exit]*

BIANCA: [Reads] *I am the Musical Scale, the ground of all accord, 'A - re,'*
to plead for Hortensio's passion; 'B - mi,' Bianca, take him as your lord,
'C - fa - ut,' that loves you with all affection; 'D - sol - re,' one clef, two
notes have I; 'E - la - mi,' show pity, or I die. You call this a musical
scale? Hmph, I don't like it. Old fashions please me best. I'm not so
changeable that you have to change true rules for odd inventions.

[A Servant enters]

SERVANT: Mistress, your father asks you to leave your books and help to
clean up your sister's bedroom. You know tomorrow is the wedding day.

BIANCA: Farewell, both of my sweet teachers. I must be gone.
                                        [Bianca and Servant exit]

LUCENTIO: In truth, mistress, then I have no cause to stay. [Lucentio exits]

HORTENSIO: But I have cause to question this teacher. I think he looks as
though he were in love, and, if your thoughts, Bianca, are so humble that
you cast your wandering eyes on every false suitor, let anyone who
wants to capture you. If I find you untrue just once, Hortensio will end
it with you by changing you for someone else.   [Hortensio exits]

Scene 2
Padua. Before Baptista's house.

[Enter Baptista, Gremio, Tranio, Katherine, Bianca, Lucentio, and others, attendants]

BAP: *[To Tranio]* Signior Lucentio, this is the 'pointed day
      That Katherine and Petruchio should be married,
      And yet we hear not of our son-in-law.
      What will be said? what mockery will it be,
5   To want the bridegroom when the priest attends
      To speak the ceremonial rites of marriage!
      What says Lucentio to this shame of ours?

KAT: No shame but mine: I must, forsooth, be forced
      To give my hand opposed against my heart
      Unto a mad-brain rudesby full of spleen;
10   Who woo'd in haste and means to wed at leisure.
      I told you, I, he was a frantic fool,
      Hiding his bitter jests in blunt behavior:
      And, to be noted for a merry man,
      He'll woo a thousand, 'point the day of marriage,
      Make feasts, invite friends, and proclaim the banns;
      Yet never means to wed where he hath woo'd.
15   Now must the world point at poor Katherine,
      And say, 'Lo, there is mad Petruchio's wife,
      If it would please him come and marry her!'

TRA: Patience, good Katherine, and Baptista too.
      Upon my life, Petruchio means but well,
      Whatever fortune stays him from his word:
20   Though he be blunt, I know him passing wise;
      Though he be merry, yet withal he's honest.

KAT: Would Katherine had never seen him though!
               [Exit weeping, followed by Bianca and others]

SCENE 2
Padua. Before Baptista's house.

[Enter Baptista, Gremio, Tranio, Katherine, Bianca, Lucentio, and others, attendants]

BAPTISTA: [To Tranio] *Signior Lucentio, this is the appointed day that Katherine and Petruchio should be married. Yet we do not hear from our son-in-law. What will be said? What kind of mockery will it be, to be lacking the bridegroom when the priest shows up to speak the ceremonial rites of marriage! What does Lucentio say to this shame of ours?*

KATHERINE: *No shame but mine. I must, in truth, be forced to give my hand, which is opposed by my heart, to an insane, rude fellow full of mad impulsiveness, a man who wooed in haste and means to wed at his leisure. I told you, I did, that he was a frantic fool, hiding his bitter jests with rude behavior. He is known as a merry man, who'll woo a thousand maids, appoint the day of the marriage, make feasts, invite friends, and announce the wedding in the church. Yet he never means to wed where he has wooed. Now the world will point at poor Katherine, and say, "Look, there is mad Petruchio's wife, if it would please him to come and marry her!"*

TRANIO: *Patience, good Katherine, and Baptista, too. I swear Petruchio means well, whatever stops him from keeping his word. Though he is blunt, I know he is very wise; though he is merry, all in all, he's honest.*

KATHERINE: *I wish I had never seen him, though!*
                    [Exit weeping, followed by Bianca and others]

107

BAP: Go, girl; I cannot blame thee now to weep;
For such an injury would vex a very saint,
25   Much more a shrew of thy impatient humour.

[Enter Biondello]

BIO: Master, master! news, old news, and such news as you never heard of!

BAP: Is it new and old too? how may that be?

BIO: Why, is it not news, to hear of Petruchio's coming?

30 BAP: Is he come?

BIO: Why, no, sir.

BAP: What then?

BIO: He is coming.

BAP: When will he be here?

35 BIO: When he stands where I am and sees you there.

TRA: But say, what to thine old news?

BIO: Why, Petruchio is coming in a new hat and an old jerkin, a pair of old breeches thrice turned, a pair of boots that have been candle-cases, one buckled, another laced, an old rusty
40   sword ta'en out of the town-armory, with a broken hilt, and chapeless; with two broken points: his horse hipped with an old mothy saddle and stirrups of no kindred; besides, possessed with the glanders and like to mose in the chine; troubled with the lampass, infected with the fashions, full of wind-galls,
45   sped with spavins, rayed with yellows, past cure of the fives, stark spoiled with the staggers, begnawn with the bots, swayed in the back and shoulder-shotten; near-legged before and with

BAPTISTA: *Leave, girl. I cannot blame you for weeping now, for such an insult would trouble a saint, and it would be much more troubling to a shrew with your impatience.*

[Biondello enters]

BIONDELLO: *Master, master! News, old news, and such news as you never heard!*

BAPTISTA: *Is it new and old too? How is that?*

BIONDELLO: *Is it not news to hear of Petruchio's coming?*

BAPTISTA: *Is he here?*

BIONDELLO: *Why, no, sir.*

BAPTISTA: *What then?*

BIONDELLO: *He is coming.*

BAPTISTA: *When will he be here?*

BIONDELLO: *When he stands where I am and sees you there.*

TRANIO: *But what about your old news?*

BIONDELLO: *Petruchio is coming in a new hat and an old jacket, a pair of old pants turned inside out three times, a pair of boots that have been used as candle-cases, one buckled, another laced, an old rusty sword taken out of the town armory, with a broken hilt, and no metal point on it; with two broken laces to hold up his stockings; his horse is lame with an old moth-eaten saddle and stirrups that don't match. Besides, the horse has a runny nose, swollen glands, and a decaying backbone, troubled with a swollen mouth, infected with ulcers on its legs, full of tumors, ruined by inflamed cartilage, jaundiced, past the cure of swelling below its ears, entirely spoiled and staggering around, eaten up by intestinal worms, swayed in the back and lame-shouldered, knock-kneed forelegs, and*

50   a half-chequed bit and a head-stall of sheep's leather which,
being restrained to keep him from stumbling, hath been often
burst and now repaired with knots; one girth six time pieced
and a woman's crupper of velure, which hath two letters for her
name fairly set down in studs, and here and there pieced with
packthread.

BAP: Who comes with him?

55   BIO: O, sir, his lackey, for all the world caparisoned like the
horse; with a linen stock on one leg and a kersey boot-hose
on the other, gartered with a red and blue list; an old hat and
'the humour of forty fancies' pricked in't for a feather: a monster, a very monster in apparel, and not like a Christian foot-
60   boy or a gentleman's lackey.

TRA: 'Tis some odd humour pricks him to this fashion;
Yet oftentimes he goes but mean-apparell'd.

BAP: I am glad he's come, howsoe'er he comes.

BIO: Why, sir, he comes not.

65   BAP: Didst thou not say he comes?

BIO: Who? that Petruchio came?

BAP: Ay, that Petruchio came.

BIO: No, sir, I say his horse comes, with him on his back.

BAP: Why, that's all one.

70   BIO: Nay, by Saint Jamy,
I hold you a penny,
A horse and a man
Is more than one,
And yet not many.

110

with a broken bit and a bridle of cheap sheep's leather which, being restrained to keep him from stumbling, has often burst and is now repaired with knots; one piece has been put together six times, and with a woman's velour saddle strap, which has two letters for her name set down in studs, and here and there held together with string.

BAPTISTA: Who comes with him?

BIONDELLO: Oh, sir, his lackey, outfitted like the horse for all the world to see. A linen stocking on one leg and a coarse wool stocking on the other, each gartered with a red and blue border; an old hat with a tremendously silly feather pricked into it. A monster, a monster in apparel, and not like a Christian footboy or a gentleman's lackey.

TRANIO: It is some odd state that stirs him to wear this fashion, yet he very often goes about in common clothing.

BAPTISTA: I am glad he's come, however he comes.

BIONDELLO: Why, sir, he doesn't come.

BAPTISTA: Didn't you just say he comes?

BIONDELLO: Who? That Petruchio came?

BAPTISTA: Yes, that Petruchio came.

BIONDELLO: No, sir, I say his horse comes, with him on his back.

BAPTISTA: Why, that's all the same thing.

BIONDELLO: No, by Saint Jamy, I'll wager a penny that a horse and a man is more than one, and yet not many.

[Enter Petruchio and Grumio]

75 PET: Come, where be these gallants? who's at home?

BAP: You are welcome, sir.

PET: And yet I come not well.

BAP: And yet you halt not.

TRA: Not so well apparell'd
80   As I wish you were.

PET: Were it better, I should rush in thus.
        But where is Kate? where is my lovely bride?
        How does my father? Gentles, methinks you frown:
        And wherefore gaze this goodly company,
85   As if they saw some wondrous monument,
        Some comet or unusual prodigy?

BAP: Why, sir, you know this is your wedding-day:
        First were we sad, fearing you would not come;
        Now sadder, that you come so unprovided.
90   Fie, doff this habit, shame to your estate,
        An eye-sore to our solemn festival!

TRA: And tell us, what occasion of import
        Hath all so long detain'd you from your wife,
        And sent you hither so unlike yourself?

95 PET: Tedious it were to tell, and harsh to hear:
        Sufficeth, I am come to keep my word,
        Though in some part enforced to digress;
        Which, at more leisure, I will so excuse
        As you shall well be satisfied withal.
100   But where is Kate? I stay too long from her:
        The morning wears, 'tis time we were at church.

112

[Petruchio and Grumio enter]

PETRUCHIO: *Come, where are these gallant gentlemen? Who's at home?*

BAPTISTA: *You are welcome, sir.*

PETRUCHIO: *Yet I don't come well.*

BAPTISTA: *Yet you don't limp.*

TRANIO: *You are not so well dressed as I wish you were.*

PETRUCHIO: *Would it be better, if I should rush in. But where is Kate? Where is my lovely bride? How is my father? Gentlemen, I think you frown. Why does this good company gaze, as if they saw some wondrous monument, some comet or unusual wonder?*

BAPTISTA: *Why, sir, you know this is your wedding day. First, we were sad, fearing you would not come. Now we are sadder, that you came so unprepared. Ugh, take off these shameful clothes; they are an eyesore to our public festival!*

TRANIO: *Tell us, what important occasion has detained you so long and sent you here so unlike yourself?*

PETRUCHIO: *It would be tedious to tell and harsh to hear. Suffice it to say that I am here to keep my word, though in some part, I am forced to digress. When we have more time, I will explain so well that you will be completely satisfied by it. But where is Kate? I stay away from her too long. The morning wears away. It is time we were at church.*

TRA: See not your bride in these unreverent robes:
     Go to my chamber; put on clothes of mine.

PET: Not I, believe me: thus I'll visit her.

105 BAP: But thus, I trust, you will not marry her.

PET: Good sooth, even thus; therefore ha' done with words:
     To me she's married, not unto my clothes:
     Could I repair what she will wear in me,
     As I can change these poor accoutrements,
110   'Twere well for Kate and better for myself.
     But what a fool am I to chat with you,
     When I should bid good morrow to my bride,
     And seal the title with a lovely kiss!
                [Exeunt Petruchio and Grumio]

TRA: He hath some meaning in his mad attire:
115   We will persuade him, be it possible,
     To put on better ere he go to church.

BAP: I'll after him, and see the event of this.
          [Exeunt Baptista, Gremio, and attendants]

TRA: But to her love concerneth us to add
     Her father's liking: which to bring to pass,
120   As I before imparted to your worship,
     I am to get a man,—whate'er he be,
     It skills not much, we'll fit him to our turn,—
     And he shall be Vincentio of Pisa;
     And make assurance here in Padua
125   Of greater sums than I have promised.
     So shall you quietly enjoy your hope,
     And marry sweet Bianca with consent.

LUC: Were it not that my fellow-schoolmaster
     Doth watch Bianca's steps so narrowly,
130   'twere good, methinks, to steal our marriage;

114

TRANIO: *Don't see your bride in these irreverent robes. Go to my room. Put on clothes of mine.*

PETRUCHIO: *Not I, believe me. I'll visit her like this.*

BAPTISTA: *But like this, I trust, you will not marry her.*

PETRUCHIO: *In truth, even like this. Therefore, stop talking about it. She's married to me, not to my clothes. If I could repair what she will wear out in me like I can change this clothing, it would be good for Kate and better for myself. But what a fool I am to chat with you, when I should bid good morning to my bride, and seal the agreement with a lovely kiss!*
[Petruchio and Grumio exit]

TRANIO: *He has some meaning in his mad attire. We will persuade him, if it is possible, to put on better before he goes to church.*

BAPTISTA: *I'll go after him and see the outcome of this.*
[Baptista, Gremio, and attendants exit]

TRANIO: *But to Bianca's love we must add her father's liking; which to bring to pass, as I explained to you before, Lucentio, I am to get a man (whatever he is, it doesn't matter much; we'll make him fit our plans), and he shall be 'Vincentio of Pisa,' and make guarantees here in Padua greater than I have promised. So you will quietly enjoy your hope and marry sweet Bianca with Baptista's consent.*

LUCENTIO: *If it weren't for my fellow-schoolteacher, who watches Bianca's steps so closely, it would be good, I think, to elope. Once that happens, she'll be mine, even if the world says no.*

Which once perform'd, let all the world say no,
I'll keep mine own, despite of all the world.

TRA: That by degrees we mean to look into,
       And watch our vantage in this business:
135   We'll over-reach the greybeard, Gremio,
       The narrow-prying father, Minola,
       The quaint musician, amorous Licio;
       All for my master's sake, Lucentio.

[Re-enter Gremio]
       Signior Gremio, came you from the church?

140 GRE: As willingly as e'er I came from school.

     TRA: And is the bride and bridegroom coming home?

     GRE: A bridegroom say you? 'Tis a groom indeed,
            A grumbling groom, and that the girl shall find.

     TRA: Curster than she? why, 'tis impossible.

145 GRE: Why he's a devil, a devil, a very fiend.

     TRA: Why, she's a devil, a devil, the devil's dam.

     GRE: Tut, she's a lamb, a dove, a fool to him!
            I'll tell you, Sir Lucentio: when the priest
            Should ask, if Katherine should be his wife,
150   'Ay, by gogs-wouns,' quoth he; and swore so loud,
            That, all-amazed, the priest let fall the book;
            And, as he stoop'd again to take it up,
            The mad-brain'd bridegroom took him such a cuff
            That down fell priest and book, and book and priest:
155   'Now take them up,' quoth he, 'if any list.'

     TRA: What said the wench when he rose again?

TRANIO: We should look into an elopement and watch for our advantage. We'll dupe the ancient Gremio, the prying father, Minola, the clever musician, amorous Licio, all for my master's sake, Lucentio.

[Re-enter Gremio]
Signior Gremio, did you come from the church?

GREMIO: As willingly as I ever came from school.

TRANIO: Are the bride and bridegroom coming home?

GREMIO: A bridegroom, say you? He is a groom indeed; a grumbling groom, and the girl will find that out.

TRANIO: He's more cross than she is? Why, that's impossible.

GREMIO: He's a devil, a devil, a real fiend.

TRANIO: Why, she's a devil, a devil, the devil's mother.

GREMIO: No! She's a lamb, a dove, a fool for him! I'll tell you, Sir Lucentio, when the priest asked if Katherine should be his wife, he said, 'Yes, by God's Wounds,' and swore so loud that, all amazed, the priest let the Bible fall and as he stooped again to pick it up, the mad-brained bridegroom gave him such a cuff that down fell the priest. 'Now pick them up,' he said, 'if anybody wants to try.'

TRANIO: What did the wench say when he rose again?

GRE: Trembled and shook; for why, he stamp'd and swore,
            As if the vicar meant to cozen him.
            But after many ceremonies done,
160   He calls for wine: 'A health!' quoth he, as if
            He had been aboard, carousing to his mates
            After a storm; quaff'd off the muscadel
            And threw the sops all in the sexton's face;
            Having no other reason
165   But that his beard grew thin and hungerly
            And seem'd to ask him sops as he was drinking.
            This done, he took the bride about the neck
            And kiss'd her lips with such a clamorous smack
            That at the parting all the church did echo:
170   And I seeing this came thence for very shame;
            And after me, I know, the rout is coming.
            Such a mad marriage never was before:
            Hark, hark! I hear the minstrels play.   *[Music]*

[Re-enter Petruchio, Katherine, Bianca, Baptista, Hortensio, Grumio, and Train]

PET: Gentlemen and friends, I thank you for your pains:
175   I know you think to dine with me to-day,
            And have prepared great store of wedding cheer;
            But so it is, my haste doth call me hence,
            And therefore here I mean to take my leave.

BAP: Is't possible you will away to-night?

180 PET: I must away to-day, before night come:
            Make it no wonder; if you knew my business,
            You would entreat me rather go than stay.
            And, honest company, I thank you all,
            That have beheld me give away myself
185   To this most patient, sweet and virtuous wife:
            Dine with my father, drink a health to me;
            For I must hence; and farewell to you all.

GREMIO: *She trembled and shook. Why? Because he stamped and swore, as if the priest meant to cheat him. But after many ceremonies were done, he called for wine. 'A health!' he said, as if he had been aboard a ship, carousing with his shipmates after a storm; he drank the wine and threw the remains right in the sexton's face. He had no other reason except that his beard was thin and hungry looking and seemed to ask him for cake as he was drinking. This done, he took the bride around the neck and kissed her lips with such a noisy smack that at the parting of the kiss, all the church echoed with it. I, seeing this, left there because it was a shame, and after me, I know, the crowd is coming. There never was such a mad marriage before. Listen, listen! I hear the minstrels play.*

[Music plays]

[Re-enter Petruchio, Katherine, Bianca, Baptista, Hortensio, Grumio, and others]

PETRUCHIO: *Gentlemen and friends, I thank you for your trouble. I know you think that you should dine with me today and have prepared great amounts of wedding cheer, but my haste calls me and, therefore, I must leave.*

BAPTISTA: *Is it possible you will go away tonight?*

PETRUCHIO: *I must go away today, before night comes. Don't wonder at it. If you knew my business, you would ask me to go rather than stay. And, honest company, I thank all of you who have seen me give myself away to this patient, sweet, and virtuous wife. Dine with my father and drink to my health, for I must go from here. Farewell to you all.*

TRA: Let us entreat you stay till after dinner.

PET: It may not be.

190 GRE: Let me entreat you.

PET: It cannot be.

KAT: Let me entreat you.

PET: I am content.

KAT: Are you content to stay?

195 PET: I am content you shall entreat me stay;
But yet not stay, entreat me how you can.

KAT: Now, if you love me, stay.

PET: Grumio, my horse.

GRU: Ay, sir, they be ready: the oats have eaten the horses.

200 KAT: Nay, then,
Do what thou canst, I will not go to-day;
No, nor to-morrow, not till I please myself.
The door is open, sir; there lies your way;
You may be jogging whiles your boots are green;
205 For me, I'll not be gone till I please myself:
'Tis like you'll prove a jolly surly groom,
That take it on you at the first so roundly.

PET: O Kate, content thee; prithee, be not angry.

KAT: I will be angry: what hast thou to do?
210 Father, be quiet; he shall stay my leisure.

GRE: Ay, marry, sir, now it begins to work.

TRANIO: *Let us ask you to stay until after dinner.*

PETRUCHIO: *It may not be.*

GREMIO: *Let me entreat you.*

PETRUCHIO: *It cannot be.*

KATHERINE: *Let me entreat you.*

PETRUCHIO: *I am content.*

KATHERINE: *Are you content to stay?*

PETRUCHIO: *I am content that you will entreat me to stay; but I will not stay, no matter how you entreat me.*

KATHERINE: *Now, if you love me, stay.*

PETRUCHIO: *Grumio, my horses.*

GRUMIO: *Yes, sir, they are ready; the oats have been eaten by the horses.*

KATHERINE: *No, then, do what you can; I will not go today; no, nor tomorrow, not until I please myself. The door is open, sir. There lies your way. You may be going while your boots are still fresh. As for me, I won't be gone until I please myself. It's likely you'll turn out to be a jolly, surly groom because you are so commanding so soon.*

PETRUCHIO: *Oh, Kate, be content. I hope you will not be angry.*

KATHERINE: *I will be angry. What are you going to do about it?* [Baptista tries to speak] *Father, be quiet. He will wait until I'm ready.*

GREMIO: *Yes, indeed, sir; now it begins to work.*

KAT: Gentlemen, forward to the bridal dinner:
      I see a woman may be made a fool,
      If she had not a spirit to resist.

215 PET: They shall go forward, Kate, at thy command.
          Obey the bride, you that attend on her;
          Go to the feast, revel and domineer,
          Carouse full measure to her maidenhead,
          Be mad and merry, or go hang yourselves:
220   But for my bonny Kate, she must with me.
          Nay, look not big, nor stamp, nor stare, nor fret;
          I will be master of what is mine own:
          She is my goods, my chattels; she is my house,
          My household stuff, my field, my barn,
225   My horse, my ox, my ass, my any thing;
          And here she stands, touch her whoever dare;
          I'll bring mine action on the proudest he
          That stops my way in Padua. Grumio,
          Draw forth thy weapon, we are beset with thieves;
230   Rescue thy mistress, if thou be a man.
          Fear not, sweet wench, they shall not touch thee, Kate:
          I'll buckler thee against a million.
                    [Exeunt Petruchio, Katherine, and Grumio]

BAP: Nay, let them go, a couple of quiet ones.

GRE: Went they not quickly, I should die with laughing.

235 TRA: Of all mad matches never was the like.

LUC: Mistress, what's your opinion of your sister?

BIA: That, being mad herself, she's madly mated.

GRE: I warrant him, Petruchio is Kated.

BAP: Neighbours and friends, though bride and bridegroom
240   wants

122

KATHERINE: *Gentlemen, forward to the bridal dinner. I see a woman may be made a fool of if she doesn't have a spirit to resist.*

PETRUCHIO: *They shall go forward, Kate, at your command. Obey the bride, you who attend her. Go to the feast to revel, party well, and carouse as fully as you can to her virginity. Be mad and merry, or go hang yourselves. But, as for my bonny Kate, she must go with me. No, do not look defiant, or stamp, or stare, or fret; I will be master of what is my own. She is my goods, my property; she is my house, my household stuff, my field, my barn, my horse, my ox, my ass, my anything. Here she stands; whoever dares to touch her, I'll bring an attack on the proudest person that stops my way here in Padua. Grumio, draw your weapon; we are set upon by thieves. Rescue your mistress, if you are a man! Fear not, sweet wench, they shall not touch you, Kate. I'll shield you against a million.*

[Petruchio, Katherine, and Grumio exit]

BAPTISTA: *No, let them go. They are a couple of quiet ones.*

GREMIO: *If they had not gone quickly, I would have died from laughing.*

TRANIO: *Out of all the mad matches, there never was one like this.*

LUCENTIO: *Mistress, what's your opinion of your sister?*

BIANCA: *Being mad herself, she's madly mated.*

GREMIO: *I'll grant him, Petruchio is Kated.*

BAPTISTA: *Neighbors and friends, though the bride and bridegroom are not here to fill their places at the table, you know we are not lacking sweet-*

For to supply the places at the table,
You know there wants no junkets at the feast.
Lucentio, you shall supply the bridegroom's place:
And let Bianca take her sister's room.

245 TRA: Shall sweet Bianca practise how to bride it?

BAP: She shall, Lucentio. Come, gentlemen, let's go.

[Exeunt]

meats at the feast. Lucentio, you shall fill in for the bridegroom, and let Bianca take her sister's place.

TRANIO: *Shall sweet Bianca practice how to be a bride?*

BAPTISTA: *She shall, Lucentio. Come, gentlemen, let's go.*

[ALL exit]

ACT IV

Scene 1
Petruchio's country house.

[Enter Grumio]

GRU: Fie, fie on all tired jades, on all mad masters, and all foul ways! Was ever man so beaten? was ever man so rayed? was ever man so weary? I am sent before to make a fire, and they are coming after to warm them. Now, were not I a little pot and soon hot, my very lips might freeze to my teeth, my tongue to the roof of my mouth, my heart in my belly, ere I should come by a fire to thaw me: but I, with blowing the fire, shall warm myself; for, considering the weather, a taller man than I will take cold. Holla, ho! Curtis!

[Enter Curtis]

CUR: Who is that calls so coldly?

GRU: A piece of ice: if thou doubt it, thou mayst slide from my shoulder to my heel with no greater a run but my head and my neck. A fire, good Curtis.

CUR: Is my master and his wife coming, Grumio?

GRU: O, ay, Curtis, ay: and therefore fire, fire; cast on no water.

CUR: Is she so hot a shrew as she's reported?

ACT IV

SCENE 1
Petruchio's country house.

[Enter Grumio]

GRUMIO: *Shame! Shame on all tired, broken-down horses, on all mad masters, and all dirty roads! Was there ever a man so beaten? Was there ever a man so dirty? Was there ever a man so weary? I was sent to make a fire, and they are coming afterwards to warm themselves. If I wasn't a little guy and easily warmed, my lips might freeze to my teeth, my tongue to the roof of my mouth, and my heart in my belly before I would come across a fire to thaw me. But I, by blowing on the fire, will warm myself. Considering the weather, a taller man than I will get cold. Hello, there! Curtis!*

[Curtis enters]

CURTIS: *Who is it that calls so coldly?*

GRUMIO: *A piece of ice. If you doubt it, you may slide all the way from my shoulder to my heel with no more effort than a run from my head and my neck. Start a fire, good Curtis.*

CURTIS: *Are my master and his wife coming, Grumio?*

GRUMIO: *Oh, yes, Curtis, yes, and, therefore, fire, fire! Don't use any water.*

CURTIS: *Is she as hot a shrew as she's reported?*

GRU: She was, good Curtis, before this frost: but, thou knowest, winter tames man, woman, and beast; for it hath tamed my old master and my new mistress and myself, fellow Curtis.

20 CUR: Away, you three-inch fool! I am no beast.

GRU: Am I but three inches? why, thy horn is a foot; and so long am I at the least. But wilt thou make a fire, or shall I complain on thee to our mistress, whose hand, she being now at hand, thou shalt soon feel, to thy cold comfort, for being slow in thy
25 hot office?

CUR: I prithee, good Grumio, tell me, how goes the world?

GRU: A cold world, Curtis, in every office but thine; and therefore fire: do thy duty, and have thy duty; for my master and mistress are almost frozen to death.

30 CUR: There's fire ready; and therefore, good Grumio, the news.

GRU: Why, 'Jack, boy! ho! boy!' and as much news as will thaw.

CUR: Come, you are so full of cony-catching!

GRU: Why, therefore fire; for I have caught extreme cold. Where's the cook? is supper ready, the house trimmed, rushes strewed,
35 cobwebs swept; the serving-men in their new fustian, their white stockings, and every officer his wedding-garment on? Be the jacks fair within, the jills fair without, the carpets laid, and every thing in order?

CUR: All ready; and therefore, I pray thee, news.

40 GRU: First, know, my horse is tired; my master and mistress fallen out.

CUR: How?

GRUMIO: *She was, good Curtis, before this frost. But, you know, winter tames man, woman, and beast, for it has tamed my old master and my new mistress and myself, fellow Curtis.*

CURTIS: *Away, you three-inch fool! I'm not a beast.*

GRUMIO: *Am I only three inches tall? Why, your cuckold's horn is a foot long, and I am at least that tall. Will you make a fire, or should I complain about you to our mistress, whose hand (she is now at hand) you will soon feel, to comfort you with cold, for being slow in your hot duty of making a fire?*

CURTIS: *I beg of you, good Grumio, tell me, how goes the world?*

GRUMIO: *A cold world, Curtis, in every duty but yours and, therefore, fire. Do your duty, and get what is coming to you, for my master and mistress are almost frozen to death.*

CURTIS: *There's fire ready. And, therefore, good Grumio, the news?*

GRUMIO: *Why, "Jack, boy! ho! boy!" and as much news as can thaw.*

CURTIS: *Come, you are so full of rabbit-catching nonsense!*

GRUMIO: *Why, make fire, for I have caught extreme cold. Where's the cook? Is supper ready, the house trimmed, rushes strewn on the floor, cobwebs swept, the servingmen in their new work clothes and their white stockings? Does every servant have his wedding-garment on? Are the leather cups inside, the metal cups outside, the carpets laid, and everything in order?*

CURTIS: *All ready. And, therefore, I beg of you, tell me news.*

GRUMIO: *First, know my horse is tired, my master and mistress fallen.*

CURTIS: *How?*

Gru: Out of their saddles into the dirt; and thereby hangs a tale.

Cur: Let's ha't, good Grumio.

45 Gru: Lend thine ear.

Cur: Here.

Gru: There. *[Strikes him]*

Cur: This is to feel a tale, not to hear a tale.

Gru: And therefore 'tis called a sensible tale: and this cuff was but
50   to knock at your ear, and beseech listening. Now I begin:
      Imprimis, we came down a foul hill, my master riding behind
      my mistress,—

Cur: Both of one horse?

Gru: What's that to thee?

55 Cur: Why, a horse.

Gru: Tell thou the tale: but hadst thou not crossed me, thou
      shouldst have heard how her horse fell and she under her
      horse; thou shouldst have heard in how miry a place, how she
      was bemoiled, how he left her with the horse upon her, how he
60   beat me because her horse stumbled, how she waded through
      the dirt to pluck him off me, how he swore, how she prayed,
      that never prayed before, how I cried, how the horses ran away,
      how her bridle was burst, how I lost my crupper, with many
      things of worthy memory, which now shall die in oblivion and
65   thou return unexperienced to thy grave.

Cur: By this reckoning he is more shrew than she.

Gru: Ay; and that thou and the proudest of you all shall find
      when he comes home. But what talk I of this? Call forth

GRUMIO: Out of their saddles and into the dirt, and there is the tale.

CURTIS: Let's have it, good Grumio.

GRUMIO: Lend me your ear.

CURTIS: Here.

GRUMIO: There. [Strikes him]

CURTIS: This is to feel a tale, not to hear a tale.

GRUMIO: And, therefore, it is called a "sense"-ible tale. And this cuff was but to knock at your ear and ask you to listen. Now I begin: In the first place, we came down a dirty hill, my master riding behind my mistress,—

CURTIS: Both of them on one horse?

GRUMIO: What's that to you?

CURTIS: Why, a horse.

GRUMIO: You tell the tale! Now, if you had not made me so angry, you would have heard how her horse fell and she fell under her horse; you would have heard in how swampy a place, how she was befuddled, how he left her with the horse on top of her, how he beat me because her horse stumbled, how she waded through the dirt to pluck him off me, how he swore, how she prayed (she who never prayed before), how I cried, how the horses ran away, how her bridle was broken, how I lost my saddle strap, along with many things of worthy memory, which now shall die in oblivion, and now you will return to your grave without hearing about this experience.

CURTIS: By this tale, he is more of a shrew than she.

GRUMIO: Yes, you and the proudest of you all shall find that when he comes home. But why do I talk of this? Call forth Nathaniel, Joseph, Nicholas,

Nathaniel, Joseph, Nicholas, Philip, Walter, Sugarsop and the
70   rest: let their heads be sleekly combed, their blue coats
brushed, and their garters of an indifferent knit: let them
curtsy with their left legs and not presume to touch a hair of
my master's horse-tail till they kiss their hands. Are they all
ready?

75   CUR: They are.

GRU: Call them forth.

CUR: Do you hear, ho? you must meet my master to countenance
my mistress.

GRU: Why, she hath a face of her own.

80   CUR: Who knows not that?

GRU: Thou, it seems, that calls for company to countenance her.

CUR: I call them forth to credit her.

GRU: Why, she comes to borrow nothing of them.

[Enter four or five Serving-men]

NAT: Welcome home, Grumio!

85   PHI: How now, Grumio!

JOS: What, Grumio!

NIC: Fellow Grumio!

NAT: How now, old lad?

GRU: Welcome, you;—how now, you;— what, you;—fellow,
90   you;—and thus much for greeting. Now, my spruce companions, is all ready, and all things neat?

132

Philip, Walter, Sugarsop, and the rest. Let their heads be sleekly combed, their blue coats brushed, and their garters of matching color. Let them curtsy with their left legs and not presume to touch a hair of my master's horsetail till they show respect by kissing their hands. Are they all ready?

CURTIS: *They are.*

GRUMIO: *Call them here.*

CURTIS: *Do you hear, hello? You must meet my master and face my mistress.*

GRUMIO: *Why? She has a face of her own.*

CURTIS: *Who doesn't know that?*

GRUMIO: *You, it seems. You call for company to face her.*

CURTIS: *I call them to give credit to her.*

GRUMIO: *Why? She comes to borrow nothing from them.*

[Four or five Servants enter]

NATHANIEL: *Welcome home, Grumio!*

PHILIP: *How's it going, Grumio?*

JOSEPH: *What's up, Grumio!*

NICHOLAS: *Fellow servant, Grumio!*

NATHANIEL: *How are you, old lad?*

GRUMIO: *Welcome, you! How's it going, you? What's up, you! Fellow servant, you! That's all for greeting. Now, my well-dressed companions, is all ready and all things neat?*

133

Nat: All things is ready. How near is our master?

Gru: E'en at hand, alighted by this; and therefore be not—Cock's passion, silence! I hear my master.

[Enter Petruchio and Katherine]

95 Pet: Where be these knaves? What, no man at door
To hold my stirrup nor to take my horse!
Where is Nathaniel, Gregory, Philip?

All Serving-Men: Here, here, sir; here, sir.

Pet: Here, sir! here, sir! here, sir! here, sir!
100 You logger-headed and unpolish'd grooms!
What, no attendance? no regard? no duty?
Where is the foolish knave I sent before?

Gru: Here, sir; as foolish as I was before.

Pet: You peasant swain! you whoreson malt-horse drudge!
105 Did I not bid thee meet me in the park,
And bring along these rascal knaves with thee?

Gru: Nathaniel's coat, sir, was not fully made,
And Gabriel's pumps were all unpink'd i' the heel;
There was no link to colour Peter's hat,
110 And Walter's dagger was not come from sheathing:
There were none fine but Adam, Ralph, and Gregory;
The rest were ragged, old, and beggarly;
Yet, as they are, here are they come to meet you.

Pet: Go, rascals, go, and fetch my supper in. *[Exeunt Servants]*
115 *[Singing]* Where is the life that late I led—
Where are those—Sit down, Kate, and welcome.—
Soud, soud, soud, soud!

[Re-enter Servants with supper]

NATHANIEL: *All things are ready. How near is our master?*

GRUMIO: *Even at hand, descending from his horse. Therefore, —oh, my God, silence! I hear my master.*

[Petruchio and Katherine enter]

PETRUCHIO: *Where are these knaves? There is no man at the door to hold my stirrup nor to take my horse! Where is Nathaniel, Gregory, Phillip?*

ALL SERVING-MEN: *Here, here, sir. Here, sir.*

PETRUCHIO: *"Here, sir! Here, sir! Here, sir! Here, sir!" You blockheaded and unpolished servants! What, no attendance? No regard? No duty? Where is the foolish knave I sent before me?*

GRUMIO: *Here, sir, as foolish as I was before.*

PETRUCHIO: *You peasant good-for-nothing! You son of a whore, you stupid slave! Didn't I tell you to meet me in the park, and bring along these rascal knaves with you?*

GRUMIO: *Nathaniel's coat, sir, was not fully made, and Gabriel's shoes weren't decorated. There was no torch to color Peter's hat, and Walter's dagger has not come back from sheathing. None were fine but Adam, Ralph, and Gregory. The rest were ragged, old, and beggarly. Yet, as they are, here they have come to meet you.*

PETRUCHIO: *Go, rascals, go, and fetch my supper.*   [Servants exit]
[Petruchio sings] *Where is the life that I recently led—Where are those—Sit down, Kate, and welcome. Food, food, food, food!*

[Re-enter Servants with supper]

135

Why, when, I say? Nay, good sweet Kate, be merry.
Off with my boots, you rogues! you villains, when?
120   *[Sings]* It was the friar of orders grey,
            As he forth walked on his way:—
Out, you rogue! you pluck my foot awry:
Take that, and mend the plucking off the other. *[Strikes him]*
Be merry, Kate. Some water, here; what, ho!
Where's my spaniel Troilus? Sirrah, get you hence,
125 And bid my cousin Ferdinand come hither:
One, Kate, that you must kiss, and be acquainted with.
Where are my slippers? Shall I have some water?

[Enter one with water]
Come, Kate, and wash, and welcome heartily.
You whoreson villain! will you let it fall?   *[Strikes him]*

130 KAT: Patience, I pray you; 'twas a fault unwilling.

PET: A whoreson beetle-headed, flap-ear'd knave!
Come, Kate, sit down; I know you have a stomach.
Will you give thanks, sweet Kate; or else shall I?
What's this? mutton?

135 1ST SER: Ay.

PET: Who brought it?

PETER: I.

PET: 'Tis burnt; and so is all the meat.
What dogs are these! Where is the rascal cook?
140 How durst you, villains, bring it from the dresser,
And serve it thus to me that love it not?
There, take it to you, trenchers, cups, and all;
            [Throws the meat, &c. about the stage]
You heedless joltheads and unmanner'd slaves!
What, do you grumble? I'll be with you straight.

136

I say, when will it come? No, good sweet Kate, be merry. Off with my boots, you rogues! You villains, how long do I have to wait?
[Petruchio sings] *It was the friar of orders grey, as he walked forth on his way: Get out, you rogue! You're hurting my foot! Take that, and be careful plucking off the other boot.* [Strikes him]
Be merry, Kate. Some water, here! Come on! Where's my spaniel Troilus? Knave, get out of here, and ask my cousin Ferdinand to come here. One, Kate, that you must kiss and be acquainted with. Where are my slippers? Will someone bring me water?

[Enter one with water]
Come, Kate, and wash, and you are heartily welcome. You villainous son of a whore! Will you let the water fall? [Strikes him]

KATHERINE: *Patience, I beg you. It was an accident.*

PETRUCHIO: *A son of a whore, mallet-headed, flap-eared knave! Come, Kate, sit down. I know you're hungry. Will you give thanks, sweet Kate, or else should I? What's this? Mutton?*

FIRST SERVANT: *Yes.*

PETRUCHIO: *Who brought it?*

PETER: *I.*

PETRUCHIO: *It is burnt, and so is all the meat. What dogs these servants are! Where is the horrid cook? How dare you, villains, bring it from the kitchen table, and serve it like this to me when you know that I hate it this way? There, take it back, wooden plates, cups, and all.* [Throws the meat, plates, and cups at them] *You heedless blockheads and unmannered slaves! What, do you grumble? I'll be after you in an instant.*

137

145 KAT: I pray you, husband, be not so disquiet:
　　　 The meat was well, if you were so contented.

　　　 PET: I tell thee, Kate, 'twas burnt and dried away;
　　　　　 And I expressly am forbid to touch it,
　　　　　 For it engenders choler, planteth anger;
150　　　 And better 'twere that both of us did fast,
　　　　　 Since, of ourselves, ourselves are choleric,
　　　　　 Than feed it with such over-roasted flesh.
　　　　　 Be patient; to-morrow 't shall be mended,
　　　　　 And, for this night, we'll fast for company:
155　　　 Come, I will bring thee to thy bridal chamber.　　　*[Exeunt]*

　　　 [Re-enter Servants severally]

　　　 NAT: Peter, didst ever see the like?

　　　 PETER: He kills her in her own humour.

　　　 [Re-enter Curtis]

　　　 GRU: Where is he?

　　　 CUR: In her chamber, making a sermon of continency to her;
160　　　 And rails, and swears, and rates, that she, poor soul,
　　　　　 Knows not which way to stand, to look, to speak,
　　　　　 And sits as one new-risen from a dream.
　　　　　 Away, away! for he is coming hither.　　　*[Exeunt]*

　　　 [Re-enter Petruchio]

　　　 PET: Thus have I politicly begun my reign,
165　　　 And 'tis my hope to end successfully.
　　　　　 My falcon now is sharp and passing empty;
　　　　　 And till she stoop she must not be full-gorged,
　　　　　 For then she never looks upon her lure.
　　　　　 Another way I have to man my haggard,
170　　　 To make her come and know her keeper's call,

KATHERINE: *I beg you, husband, don't be so disturbed. The meat was fine, if you would be contented.*

PETRUCHIO: *I tell you, Kate, it was burnt and dried away, and I am not allowed to touch it, for it produces an angry disposition, plants anger, and it would be better that both of us fasted, (since between ourselves, we are prone to anger) than feed that anger with such over-roasted flesh. Be patient. Tomorrow it will be fixed, and, for tonight, we'll fast for company. Come, I will bring you to your bridal chamber.* [They exit]

[Re-enter several Servants]

NATHANIEL: *Peter, did you ever see anything like this?*

PETER: *He kills her by acting the same way she does.*

[Re-enter Curtis]

GRUMIO: *Where is he?*

CURTIS: *In her chamber, giving her a sermon on self-restraint. He yells, and swears, and berates her, so that she, poor soul, doesn't know which way to stand, to look, or to speak. She sits as someone who has just awoken from a dream. Away, away! He is coming here.* [They exit]

[Re-enter PETRUCHIO]

PETRUCHIO: *Now I have begun my reign like a shrewd politician, and it is my hope to end successfully. My falcon, Kate, is now hungry and very empty, and until she obeys, she must not be fed, or then she will never listen to what I say. Another way I have to train my falcon, to make her come and know her keeper's call, is to keep her awake, as we keep those falcons awake that flap and beat their wings and will not be obedient. She ate no meat today, and she won't eat any. Last night she didn't sleep, and*

That is, to watch her, as we watch these kites
That bate and beat and will not be obedient.
She eat no meat to-day, nor none shall eat;
Last night she slept not, nor to-night she shall not;
175   As with the meat, some undeserved fault
I'll find about the making of the bed;
And here I'll fling the pillow, there the bolster,
This way the coverlet, another way the sheets:
Ay, and amid this hurly I intend
180   That all is done in reverend care of her;
And in conclusion she shall watch all night:
And if she chance to nod I'll rail and brawl
And with the clamour keep her still awake.
This is a way to kill a wife with kindness;
185   And thus I'll curb her mad and headstrong humour.
He that knows better how to tame a shrew,
Now let him speak: 'tis charity to show.   *[Exit]*

SCENE 2

Padua. Before Baptista's house.

[Enter Tranio and Hortensio]

TRA: Is't possible, friend Licio, that Mistress Bianca
Doth fancy any other but Lucentio?
I tell you, sir, she bears me fair in hand.

HOR: Sir, to satisfy you in what I have said,
5   Stand by and mark the manner of his teaching.

[Enter Bianca and Lucentio]

LUC: Now, mistress, profit you in what you read?

BIA: What, master, read you? first resolve me that.

140

tonight she will not. Just like I said that the meat was burned, I'll find some undeserved fault about the making of the bed, and I'll fling the pillow here, the cushion there. I'll throw the coverlet this way, the sheets another way. And during this uproar I'll pretend that all this is done in reverent care of her. And, in conclusion, she'll stay awake all night, and if she nods, I'll yell and make a lot of noise and keep her awake with the clamor. This is a way to kill a wife with kindness. Thus I'll curb her mad and headstrong attitude. Anyone that knows how to better tame a shrew, let him speak now; it is charity to show me how.   [Petruchio exits]

SCENE 2
Padua. Before Baptista's house.

[Tranio and Hortensio enter]

TRANIO: *Is it possible, friend Licio, that Mistress Bianca fancies anyone else but Lucentio? I tell you, sir, she encourages me.*

HORTENSIO: *Sir, to make you believe what I have told you, stand by and watch how he teaches.*

[Bianca and Lucentio enter]

LUCENTIO: *Now, mistress, do you profit by what you read?*

BIANCA: *What are you reading, teacher? First answer that.*

141

LUC: I read that I profess, the Art to Love.

BIA: And may you prove, sir, master of your art!

10   LUC: While you, sweet dear, prove mistress of my heart!

HOR: Quick proceeders, marry! Now, tell me, I pray,
You that durst swear that your mistress Bianca
Loved none in the world so well as Lucentio.

TRA: O despiteful love! unconstant womankind!
15   I tell thee, Licio, this is wonderful.

HOR: Mistake no more: I am not Licio,
Nor a musician, as I seem to be;
But one that scorn to live in this disguise,
For such a one as leaves a gentleman,
20   And makes a god of such a cullion:
Know, sir, that I am call'd Hortensio.

TRA: Signior Hortensio, I have often heard
Of your entire affection to Bianca;
And since mine eyes are witness of her lightness,
25   I will with you, if you be so contented,
Forswear Bianca and her love for ever.

HOR: See, how they kiss and court! Signior Lucentio,
Here is my hand, and here I firmly vow
Never to woo her no more, but do forswear her,
30   As one unworthy all the former favours
That I have fondly flatter'd her withal.

TRA: And here I take the unfeigned oath,
Never to marry with her though she would entreat:
Fie on her! see, how beastly she doth court him!

35   HOR: Would all the world but he had quite forsworn!
For me, that I may surely keep mine oath,

LUCENTIO: *I read what I profess: "The Art to Love."*

BIANCA: *And sir, may you prove to be master of your art!*

LUCENTIO: *While you, sweet dear, prove mistress of my heart!*

HORTENSIO: *They are getting to the matter quickly, indeed! Now, tell me, I beg of you, you that swear that your mistress Bianca loves none in the world as well as Lucentio.*

TRANIO: *Oh, hateful love! Unfaithful womanhood! I tell you, Licio, this is wonderful.*

HORTENSIO: *Make no mistake. I am not Licio, nor a musician, as I seem to be, but one that scorns to live in this disguise. Such a person stops being a gentleman, and makes a god of such a lowly servant. Know, sir, that I am called Hortensio.*

TRANIO: *Signior Hortensio, I have often heard of your complete affection for Bianca. Since my eyes have witnessed her unfaithfulness, I will join with you, if you are so inclined, and give up Bianca and her love forever.*

HORTENSIO: *See, how they kiss and court! Signior Lucentio, here is my hand, and here I firmly vow never to woo her again; I give her up, as one who is unworthy of all the former favors that I have fondly flattered her with.*

TRANIO: *And here I take the same true oath, never to marry her even if she begs me to. Shame on her! See how shamelessly she courts him!*

HORTENSIO: *I wish that she only had one lover in the whole world! For me, so that I may surely keep my oath, before three days pass, I will be mar-*

I will be married to a wealthy widow,
Ere three days pass, which hath as long loved me
As I have loved this proud disdainful haggard.
40   And so farewell, Signior Lucentio.
Kindness in women, not their beauteous looks,
Shall win my love: and so I take my leave,
In resolution as I swore before.   *[Exit]*

TRA: Mistress Bianca, bless you with such grace
45   As 'longeth to a lover's blessed case!
Nay, I have ta'en you napping, gentle love,
And have forsworn you with Hortensio.

BIA: Tranio, you jest: but have you both forsworn me?

TRA: Mistress, we have.

50 LUC: Then we are rid of Licio.

TRA: I' faith, he'll have a lusty widow now,
That shall be woo'd and wedded in a day.

BIA: God give him joy!

TRA: Ay, and he'll tame her.

55 BIA: He says so, Tranio.

TRA: Faith, he is gone unto the taming-school.

BIA: The taming-school! what, is there such a place?

TRA: Ay, mistress, and Petruchio is the master;
That teacheth tricks eleven and twenty long,
60   To tame a shrew and charm her chattering tongue.

[Enter Biondello]

144

ried to a wealthy widow, who has loved me as long as I have loved this proud, disdainful hawk. And so farewell, Signior Lucentio. Kindness in women, not their beautiful looks, will win my love. And so I leave, resolving to do what I swore before. [Hortensio exits]

TRANIO: Mistress Bianca, bless you with such grace as belongs to a lover's blessed circumstances! I have caught you napping, gentle love, and have given up on you with Hortensio.

BIANCA: Tranio, you're joking. Have you both given up on me?

TRANIO: Mistress, we have.

LUCENTIO: Then we are rid of Licio.

TRANIO: To tell the truth, he'll have a lusty widow now, who will be wooed and wedded in a day.

BIANCA: God give him joy!

TRANIO: Yes, and he'll tame her.

BIANCA: He says so, Tranio.

TRANIO: In truth, he is gone to the taming-school.

BIANCA: The taming-school! What, is there such a place?

TRANIO: Yes, mistress, and Petruchio is the master who teaches tricks to tame a shrew exactly right and silence her chattering tongue.

[Biondello enters]

BIO: O master, master, I have watch'd so long
That I am dog-weary: but at last I spied
An ancient angel coming down the hill,
Will serve the turn.

65   TRA: What is he, Biondello?

BIO: Master, a mercatante, or a pedant,
I know not what; but formal in apparel,
In gait and countenance surely like a father.

LUC: And what of him, Tranio?

70   TRA: If he be credulous and trust my tale,
I'll make him glad to seem Vincentio,
And give assurance to Baptista Minola,
As if he were the right Vincentio.
Take in your love, and then let me alone.
                    [Exeunt Lucentio and Bianca]

[Enter a Pedant]

75   PED: God save you, sir!

TRA: And you, sir! you are welcome.
Travel you far on, or are you at the farthest?

PED: Sir, at the farthest for a week or two:
But then up farther, and as far as Rome;
80   And so to Tripoli, if God lend me life.

TRA: What countryman, I pray?

PED: Of Mantua.

TRA: Of Mantua, sir? marry, God forbid!
And come to Padua, careless of your life?

BIONDELLO: *Oh, master, master, I have watched so long that I am dog-tired, but at last I spied a reliable old man coming down the hill, who will serve us as your father.*

TRANIO: *What is he, Biondello?*

BIONDELLO: *Master, a merchant or a teacher. I know not which. The way he walks in formal clothing, and his face, is surely like a father.*

LUCENTIO: *And what about him, Tranio?*

TRANIO: *If he is easily deceived and trusts my tale, I'll make him glad to pretend to be Vincentio, and give a guarantee to Baptista Minola, as if he were the real Vincentio. Take your love inside, and then let me alone.*
[Lucentio and Bianca exit]

[A Teacher enters]

TEACHER: *God save you, sir!*

TRANIO: *And you, sir! You are welcome. Do you travel farther on, or are you at the farthest?*

TEACHER: *Sir, at the farthest in a week or two, but then I go farther, as far as Rome, and then to Tripoli, if God wills it.*

TRANIO: *What country are you from?*

TEACHER: *Mantua.*

TRANIO: *Of Mantua, sir? Indeed, God forbid! And you come to Padua, careless of your life?*

85   PED: My life, sir! how, I pray? for that goes hard.

TRA: 'Tis death for any one in Mantua
       To come to Padua. Know you not the cause?
       Your ships are stay'd at Venice, and the duke,
       For private quarrel 'twixt your duke and him,
90   Hath publish'd and proclaim'd it openly:
       'Tis marvel, but that you are but newly come,
       You might have heard it else proclaim'd about.

PED: Alas! sir, it is worse for me than so;
       For I have bills for money by exchange
95   From Florence and must here deliver them.

TRA: Well, sir, to do you courtesy,
       This will I do, and this I will advise you:
       First, tell me, have you ever been at Pisa?

PED: Ay, sir, in Pisa have I often been,
100   Pisa renowned for grave citizens.

TRA: Among them know you one Vincentio?

PED: I know him not, but I have heard of him;
       A merchant of incomparable wealth.

TRA: He is my father, sir; and, sooth to say,
105   In countenance somewhat doth resemble you.

BIO: [Aside] As much as an apple doth an oyster, and all one.

TRA: To save your life in this extremity,
       This favour will I do you for his sake;
       And think it not the worst of all your fortunes
110   That you are like to Sir Vincentio.
       His name and credit shall you undertake,
       And in my house you shall be friendly lodged:

TEACHER : *My life, sir! What do you mean? I beg you to tell me, for that is serious.*

TRANIO: *It is death for any one in Mantua to come to Padua. Do you not know why? Your ships are being held in Venice, and the duke, because of a private quarrel between your duke and him, has published and proclaimed this death sentence openly. It is a marvel, except that you have just arrived, or else you might have heard it proclaimed about.*

TEACHER: *What a pity! Sir, it is worse for me than that, because I have papers from Florence to exchange for money and I must deliver them here.*

TRANIO: *Well, sir, to do you a courtesy, I will do this, and I will advise you. First, tell me, have you ever been to Pisa?*

TEACHER: *Yes, sir, I have often been in Pisa. Pisa is well known for its serious citizens.*

TRANIO: *Do you know one man among them named Vincentio?*

TEACHER: *I don't know him, but I have heard of him; he's a merchant of incomparable wealth.*

TRANIO: *He is my father, sir, and it is truth to say that in appearance he somewhat resembles you.*

BIONDELLO: [Aside] *As much as an apple does an oyster, but no matter.*

TRANIO: *To save your life in this extreme circumstance, I will do this favor for you for his sake (and don't think it is the worst of your fortunes that you look like Sir Vincentio). You will take his name and reputation, and you will find friendly lodging in my house. Make sure you are careful about what you are doing. Understand me, sir, you will stay this way until you have done your business in the city. If this is a courtesy to you, sir, accept it.*

Look that you take upon you as you should;
You understand me, sir: so shall you stay
115   Till you have done your business in the city:
If this be courtesy, sir, accept of it.

PED: O sir, I do; and will repute you ever
The patron of my life and liberty.

TRA: Then go with me to make the matter good.
120   This, by the way, I let you understand;
my father is here look'd for every day,
To pass assurance of a dower in marriage
'Twixt me and one Baptista's daughter here:
In all these circumstances I'll instruct you:
125   Go with me to clothe you as becomes you.   *[Exeunt]*

Scene 3
A room in Petruchio's house.

[Enter Katherine and Grumio]

GRU: No, no, forsooth; I dare not for my life.

KAT: The more my wrong, the more his spite appears:
What, did he marry me to famish me?
Beggars, that come unto my father's door,
5   Upon entreaty have a present alms;
If not, elsewhere they meet with charity:
But I, who never knew how to entreat,
Nor never needed that I should entreat,
Am starved for meat, giddy for lack of sleep,
10   With oath kept waking and with brawling fed:
And that which spites me more than all these wants,
He does it under name of perfect love;
As who should say, if I should sleep or eat,

150

TEACHER: *Oh, sir, I do and will tell people everywhere that you are the patron of my life and liberty.*

TRANIO: *Then, go with me to carry out this plan. This, by the way, I'll let you understand: My father is looked for every day, to give the guarantee of an inheritance in marriage between me and Baptista's daughter here. I'll instruct you in all of these issues. Go with me to get dressed up to look like my father.* [They exit]

Scene 3
A room in Petruchio's house.

[Katherine and Grumio enter]

GRUMIO: *No, no, honestly. My life depends on it.*

KATHERINE: *The more wrong I suffer, the more his spite appears. What, did he marry me to famish me? Beggars that come to my father's door, when they ask, are quickly given money. If not, they find charity elsewhere. But I, who never knew how to beg, and never needed to beg, am kept from eating meat, dizzy from lack of sleep, kept awake with swearing and fed with brawling. That which bothers me more than all these things I'm lacking, is that he does it under the name of perfect love as if to say, if I should sleep or eat, it would be a deadly sickness or else immediate death. I beg you to go and get me some dinner. I don't care what, as long as it is wholesome food.*

'Twere deadly sickness or else present death.
15   I prithee go and get me some repast;
       I care not what, so it be wholesome food.

GRU: What say you to a neat's foot?

KAT: 'Tis passing good: I prithee let me have it.

GRU: I fear it is too choleric a meat.
20   How say you to a fat tripe finely broil'd?

KAT: I like it well: good Grumio, fetch it me.

GRU: I cannot tell; I fear 'tis choleric.
       What say you to a piece of beef and mustard?

KAT: A dish that I do love to feed upon.

25 GRU: Ay, but the mustard is too hot a little.

KAT: Why then, the beef, and let the mustard rest.

GRU: Nay then, I will not: you shall have the mustard,
       Or else you get no beef of Grumio.

KAT: Then both, or one, or any thing thou wilt.

30 GRU: Why then, the mustard without the beef.

KAT: Go, get thee gone, thou false deluding slave,   [Beats him]
       That feed'st me with the very name of meat:
       Sorrow on thee and all the pack of you,
       That triumph thus upon my misery!
35   Go, get thee gone, I say.

[Enter Petruchio and Hortensio with meat]

PET: How fares my Kate? What, sweeting, all amort?

152

GRUMIO: *What do you say to a calf's foot?*

KATHERINE: *It is very good. I beg of you, let me have it.*

GRUMIO: *I'm afraid it will make you too angry. What do you say to a fat cow stomach, finely broiled?*

KATHERINE: *I like it well. Good Grumio, fetch it for me.*

GRUMIO: *I'm not sure. I'm afraid it's also an anger-causing food. What do you say to a piece of beef with mustard?*

KATHERINE: *That's a dish that I love to eat.*

GRUMIO: *Yes, but the mustard is a little too hot.*

KATHERINE: *Why then, the beef, without the mustard.*

GRUMIO: *No then, I will not. You will have the mustard, or else you get no beef from Grumio.*

KATHERINE: *Then both, or one, or anything you will give me.*

GRUMIO: *Why, then, the mustard without the beef.*

KATHERINE: [Beats him] *Go, get out of here, you false, lying slave, who feeds me with only the name of meat. May sorrow come upon you and the whole pack of you that triumph in my misery! Go, I say, get out here.*

[Petruchio and Hortensio enter with meat]

PETRUCHIO: *How is my Kate doing? What, sweetheart, are you sick to death?*

153

HOR: Mistress, what cheer?

KAT: Faith, as cold as can be.

PET: Pluck up thy spirits; look cheerfully upon me.
40   Here love; thou see'st how diligent I am
        To dress thy meat myself and bring it thee:
        I am sure, sweet Kate, this kindness merits thanks.
        What, not a word? Nay, then thou lovest it not;
        And all my pains is sorted to no proof.
45   Here, take away this dish.

KAT: I pray you, let it stand.

PET: The poorest service is repaid with thanks;
        And so shall mine, before you touch the meat.

KAT: I thank you, sir.

50 HOR: Signior Petruchio, fie! you are to blame.
        Come, mistress Kate, I'll bear you company.

PET: [Aside] Eat it up all, Hortensio, if thou lovest me.
        Much good do it unto thy gentle heart!
        Kate, eat apace: and now, my honey love,
55   Will we return unto thy father's house
        And revel it as bravely as the best,
        With silken coats and caps and golden rings,
        With ruffs and cuffs and farthingales and things;
        With scarfs and fans and double change of bravery,
60   With amber bracelets, beads and all this knavery.
        What, hast thou dined? The tailor stays thy leisure,
        To deck thy body with his ruffling treasure.

[Enter Tailor]
        Come, tailor, let us see these ornaments;
        Lay forth the gown.

HORTENSIO: Mistress, how are you?

KATHERINE: I swear, as cold as can be.

PETRUCHIO: Raise your spirits. Look cheerfully at me. Here, love, you can see how diligent I am to prepare your meat myself and bring it you. [Sets the dish on a table] I am sure, sweet Kate, this kindness deserves thanks. What, not a word? No, then you don't love it, and all my pains have no effect on you. Here, take away this dish.

KATHERINE: I beg of you, let it stay.

PETRUCHIO: Even the poorest service is repaid with thanks, and, so, you will thank me before you touch the meat.

KATHERINE: I thank you, sir.

HORTENSIO: Signior Petruchio, shame! You are to blame. Come, mistress Kate, I'll keep you company.

PETRUCHIO: [Aside] Eat it all up, Hortensio, if you are my friend. It will do much good to your gentle heart! Kate, eat quickly. And now, my honey love, will we return to your father's house and party in as splendid clothing as the best, with silken coats and caps and golden rings, with ruffles and cuffs and petticoats and things, with scarfs and fans and double changes of clothing, with amber bracelets, beads and all this trickery. What, have you dined? The tailor is waiting for you, in order to adorn your body with his rustling treasure.

[Tailor enters]
Come, tailor, let us see these ornaments. Bring out the gown.

[Enter Haberdasher]

65   What news with you, sir?

HAB: Here is the cap your worship did bespeak.

PET: Why, this was moulded on a porringer;
        A velvet dish: fie, fie! 'tis lewd and filthy:
        Why, 'tis a cockle or a walnut-shell,
70   A knack, a toy, a trick, a baby's cap:
        Away with it! come, let me have a bigger.

KAT: I'll have no bigger: this doth fit the time,
        And gentlewomen wear such caps as these.

PET: When you are gentle, you shall have one too,
75   And not till then.

HOR: *[Aside]* That will not be in haste.

KAT: Why, sir, I trust I may have leave to speak;
        And speak I will; I am no child, no babe:
        Your betters have endured me say my mind,
80   And if you cannot, best you stop your ears.
        My tongue will tell the anger of my heart,
        Or else my heart concealing it will break,
        And rather than it shall, I will be free
        Even to the uttermost, as I please, in words.

85 PET: Why, thou say'st true; it is a paltry cap,
        A custard-coffin, a bauble, a silken pie:
        I love thee well, in that thou likest it not.

KAT: Love me or love me not, I like the cap;
        And it I will have, or I will have none.   *[Exit Haberdasher]*

90 PET: Thy gown? why, ay: come, tailor, let us see't.
        O mercy, God! what masquing stuff is here?
        What's this? a sleeve? 'tis like a demi-cannon:

[Hatmaker enters]
> What news do you have, sir?

HATMAKER: *Here is the cap your lordship spoke of.*

PETRUCHIO: *Why, this was molded on a porridge bowl! A velvet dish. Shame, shame! It is lewd and filthy. Why, it's a cockleshell or a walnut-shell, a knick-knack, a toy, a trick, a baby's cap. Take it away! Come, bring me a bigger one.*

KATHERINE: *I don't want a bigger one. This is the current fashion, gentle-women wear caps like this.*

PETRUCHIO: *When you are gentle, you shall have one too, and not until then.*

HORTENSIO: [Aside] *That won't happen quickly.*

KATHERINE: *Why, sir, I believe I may have permission to speak, and speak I will. I am no child, no baby. People better than you have endured me when I spoke my mind, and if you cannot, you better stop up your ears. My tongue will tell the anger of my heart, or else my heart will break by concealing the anger. Rather than let that happen, I will be free with speaking as much as I please.*

PETRUCHIO: *Why, what you say is true. It is a cheap cap; it's like a custard crust, a little nothing, a silken pie. I really love you, because you don't like it.*

KATHERINE: *Love me or don't love me, I like the cap, and I will have it, or I will have none.*   [Hatmaker exits]

PETRUCHIO: *Your gown? Why, yes. Come, tailor, let us see it. Oh, mercy, God! What cheap costume stuff do we have here? What's this, a sleeve? It looks like half a cannon. It's carved up and down like an apple-tart!*

What, up and down, carved like an apple-tart?
Here's snip and nip and cut and slish and slash,
95   Like to a censer in a barber's shop:
Why, what, i' devil's name, tailor, call'st thou this?

Hor: *[Aside]* I see she's like to have neither cap nor gown.

Tai: You bid me make it orderly and well,
According to the fashion and the time.

100 Pet: Marry, and did; but if you be remember'd,
I did not bid you mar it to the time.
Go, hop me over every kennel home,
For you shall hop without my custom, sir:
I'll none of it: hence! make your best of it.

105 Kat: I never saw a better-fashion'd gown,
More quaint, more pleasing, nor more commendable:
Belike you mean to make a puppet of me.

Pet: Why, true; he means to make a puppet of thee.

Tai: She says your worship means to make a puppet of her.

110 Pet: O monstrous arrogance!
Thou liest, thou thread, thou thimble,
Thou yard, three-quarters, half-yard, quarter, nail!
Thou flea, thou nit, thou winter-cricket thou!
Braved in mine own house with a skein of hread?
115   Away, thou rag, thou quantity, thou remnant;
Or I shall so be-mete thee with thy yard
As thou shalt think on prating whilst thou livest!
I tell thee, I, that thou hast marr'd her gown.

Tai: Your worship is deceived; the gown is made
120   Just as my master had direction:
Grumio gave order how it should be done.

158

Here's snip and nip and cut and slish and slash, like the incense holder in a barber's shop. Why, what in the devil's name, tailor, do you call this?

HORTENSIO: [Aside] I see she's going to have neither cap nor gown.

TAILOR: You told me to make it orderly and well, according to the fashion and the time.

PETRUCHIO: Indeed, I did. But if you remember, I did not ask you to spoil it with the time. Go, hop over every gutter home, for you will hop without me being your customer, sir. I'll not have it. Get out of here! Make the best of it.

KATHERINE: I never saw a better-fashioned gown, more quaint, more pleasing, or more commendable. Perhaps you mean to make a puppet of me.

PETRUCHIO: Why, true, the tailor means to make a puppet of you.

TAILOR: She says your lordship means to make a puppet of her.

PETRUCHIO: Oh, monstrous arrogance! You lie, you thread, you thimble, you yardstick, three-quarters of a yardstick, half, quarter, one-sixteenth of a yardstick! You flea, you nit, you winter-cricket you! Defied in my own house with a spool of thread? Away, you scrap of cloth, you fragment, you remnant, or I shall so beat you with your yardstick that you will think twice before chattering on while you live! I tell you, I do, that you have ruined her gown.

TAILOR: Your lordship is deceived. The gown is made according to the directions my master was given. Grumio gave the order how it should be done.

GRU: I gave him no order; I gave him the stuff.

TAI: But how did you desire it should be made?

GRU: Marry, sir, with needle and thread.

125 TAI: But did you not request to have it cut?

GRU: Thou hast faced many things.

TAI: I have.

GRU: Face not me: thou hast braved many men; brave not me; I
will neither be faced nor braved. I say unto thee, I bid thy
130 master cut out the gown; but I did not bid him cut it to
pieces: ergo, thou liest.

TAI: Why, here is the note of the fashion to testify.

PET: Read it.

GRU: The note lies in's throat, if he say I said so.

135 TAI: [Reads] 'Imprimis, a loose-bodied gown:'

GRU: Master, if ever I said loose-bodied gown, sew me in the
skirts of it, and beat me to death with a bottom of brown
thread: I said a gown.

PET: Proceed.

140 TAI: [Reads] 'With a small compassed cape:'

GRU: I confess the cape.

TAI: [Reads] 'With a trunk sleeve:'

GRU: I confess two sleeves.

GRUMIO: *I gave him no order; I gave him the stuff to make the gown.*

TAILOR: *But how did you desire it to be made?*

GRUMIO: *Indeed, sir, with needle and thread.*

TAILOR: *But didn't you request to have it cut?*

GRUMIO: *You have faced many things in your occupation.*

TAILOR: *I have.*

GRUMIO: *Don't face me! You have dressed many men. Don't dress me. I will be neither faced nor dressed. I say to you, I told your master to cut out the gown, but I did not tell him to cut it to pieces. Therefore, you lie.*

TAILOR: *Why, here is the note that will prove how you wanted it fashioned.*

PETRUCHIO: *Read it.*

GRUMIO: *The note lies, if it says I said to cut the dress to pieces.*

TAILOR: [Reads] *"First, a loose-bodied gown–"*

GRUMIO: *Master, if ever I said loose-bodied gown, sew me in the skirts of it, and beat me to death with a spool of brown thread. I said a gown.*

PETRUCHIO: *Proceed.*

TAILOR: [Reads] *"With a small semi-circular cape–"*

GRUMIO: *I confess to the part about the cape.*

TAILOR: [Reads] *"With a wide sleeve–"*

GRUMIO: *I confess to two sleeves.*

TAI: [*Reads*] 'The sleeves curiously cut.'

145   PET: Ay, there's the villany.

GRU: Error i' the bill, sir; error i' the bill.
I commanded the sleeves should be cut out and sewed up
again; and that I'll prove upon thee, though thy little finger be
armed in a thimble.

150   TAI: This is true that I say: an I had thee in place where, thou
shouldst know it.

GRU: I am for thee straight: take thou the bill, give me thy mete-
yard, and spare not me.

HOR: God-a-mercy, Grumio! then he shall have no odds.

155   PET: Well, sir, in brief, the gown is not for me.

GRU: You are i' the right, sir: 'tis for my mistress.

PET: Go, take it up unto thy master's use.

GRU: Villain, not for thy life: take up my mistress' gown for thy
master's use!

160   PET: Why, sir, what's your conceit in that?

GRU: O, sir, the conceit is deeper than you think for:
Take up my mistress' gown to his master's use!
O, fie, fie, fie!

PET: [*Aside*] Hortensio, say thou wilt see the tailor paid.
165   Go take it hence; be gone, and say no more.

HOR: Tailor, I'll pay thee for thy gown tomorrow:
Take no unkindness of his hasty words:
Away! I say; commend me to thy master.   [*Exit Tailor*]

TAILOR: [Reads] *"The sleeves curiously cut."*

PETRUCHIO: Ah ha! There's the villainy.

GRUMIO: Error in the note, sir, error in the note! I commanded that the sleeves should be cut out and sewed up again, and that I'll prove to you, though your little finger is armed in a thimble.

TAILOR: What I say is true. And if I had you in a place where it was proper to fight, you would know it.

GRUMIO: I'll take you on straight away. You take the note, give me your yardstick, and don't spare me.

HORTENSIO: God have mercy, Grumio! Then he will have no odds to win.

PETRUCHIO: Well, sir, in brief, the gown is not for me.

GRUMIO: You are right, sir. It is for my mistress.

PETRUCHIO: Go, take it up to your master to use.

GRUMIO: Villain, not on your life. Take up my mistress' gown for your master's use!

PETRUCHIO: Why, sir, what idea are you hinting at?

GRUMIO: Oh, sir, the idea is deeper than you think. Lift up my mistress' gown for his master's use! Oh, shame, shame, shame!

PETRUCHIO: [Aside to Hortensio] Hortensio, see that the tailor gets paid. [To Tailor] Go take it away. Be gone, and say no more.

HORTENSIO: Tailor, I'll pay you for your gown tomorrow. Take no offense at his hasty words. Away, I say! Give your master my regards.

[Tailor exits]

PET: Well, come, my Kate; we will unto your father's
170   Even in these honest mean habiliments:
         Our purses shall be proud, our garments poor;
         For 'tis the mind that makes the body rich;
         And as the sun breaks through the darkest clouds,
         So honour peereth in the meanest habit.
175   What is the jay more precious than the lark,
         Because his feathers are more beautiful?
         Or is the adder better than the eel,
         Because his painted skin contents the eye?
         O, no, good Kate; neither art thou the worse
180   For this poor furniture and mean array.
         If thou account'st it shame, lay it on me;
         And therefore frolic: we will hence forthwith,
         To feast and sport us at thy father's house.
         Go, call my men, and let us straight to him;
185   And bring our horses unto Long-lane end;
         There will we mount, and thither walk on foot.
         Let's see; I think 'tis now some seven o'clock,
         And well we may come there by dinner-time.

KAT: I dare assure you, sir, 'tis almost two;
190   And 'twill be supper-time ere you come there.

PET: It shall be seven ere I go to horse:
         Look, what I speak, or do, or think to do,
         You are still crossing it. Sirs, let't alone:
         I will not go to-day; and ere I do,
195   It shall be what o'clock I say it is.

HOR: [Aside] Why, so this gallant will command the sun.

                                             [Exeunt]

164

PETRUCHIO: *Well, come, my Kate. We will go to your father's even in these honest common clothes. Our purses will be proud, our garments poor, for it is the mind that makes the body rich. As the sun breaks through the darkest clouds, so honor appears in the most common clothing. Is the jay more precious than the lark because his feathers are more beautiful? Or is the adder better than the eel because his colorful skin pleases the eye? Oh, no, good Kate. Neither are you worse off because of this poor equipment and common clothing. If you think it is shameful, blame me, and frolic! We will go right now, to feast and be entertained at your father's house. Go, call my men, and let us go straight to him, and bring our horses to the end of Long-lane. There will we mount, and get there by walking. Let's see, I think it is now almost seven o'clock, and we may well get there by lunchtime.*

KATHERINE: *I assure you, sir, it's almost two, and it will be suppertime before you get there.*

PETRUCHIO: *It will be seven before I go to the horses. Pay attention to what I speak, or do, or think to do; you are still crossing it. Sirs, let it alone. I will not go today, and before I do, it will be whatever o'clock I say it is.*

HORTENSIO: [Aside] *Why, this is the way the high-spirited man will command the sun.*

[All exit]

Scene 4
Padua. Before Baptista's house.

[Enter Tranio, and the Pedant dressed like Vincentio]

TRA: Sir, this is the house: please it you that I call?

PED: Ay, what else? and but I be deceived
     Signior Baptista may remember me,
     Near twenty years ago, in Genoa,
5   Where we were lodgers at the Pegasus.

TRA: 'Tis well; and hold your own, in any case,
     With such austerity as 'longeth to a father.

PED: I warrant you.

[Enter Biondello]
     But, sir, here comes your boy;
10   'Twere good he were school'd.

TRA: Fear you not him. Sirrah Biondello,
     Now do your duty throughly, I advise you:
     Imagine 'twere the right Vincentio.

BIO: Tut, fear not me.

15   TRA: But hast thou done thy errand to Baptista?

BIO: I told him that your father was at Venice,
     And that you look'd for him this day in Padua.

TRA: Thou'rt a tall fellow: hold thee that to drink.
     Here comes Baptista: set your countenance, sir.

[Enter Baptista and Lucentio]

166

Scene 4
Padua. Before Baptista's house.

[Tranio as Lucentio, and the Teacher dressed as Vincentio enter]

TRANIO: *Sir, this is the house. Does it please you that I call?*

TEACHER: *Yes, what else? Unless I am deceived, Signior Baptista may remember me. It was almost twenty years ago, in Genoa, where we were lodgers at the Pegasus Inn.*

TRANIO: *That's good. And keep up the appearance of austerity, in any case, like a father.*

TEACHER: *I guarantee you.*

[Biondello enters]
But, sir, here comes your servant. It would be good if he knew what we were doing.

TRANIO: *Don't fear him. Servant Biondello, do your duty thoroughly, I advise you. Imagine that he is the real Vincentio.*

BIONDELLO: *Ah, don't fear me.*

TRANIO: *But have you done your errand to Baptista?*

BIONDELLO: *I told him that your father was in Venice, and that you looked for him today in Padua.*

TRANIO: *You're a good man. Here's some money, buy yourself a drink. Here comes Baptista. Pretend to be my father, sir.*

[Enter Baptista and Lucentio as Cambio]

20   Signior Baptista, you are happily met.
       [To the Pedant]
       Sir, this is the gentleman I told you of:
       I pray you stand good father to me now,
       Give me Bianca for my patrimony.

     PED: Soft, son!
25   Sir, by your leave: having come to Padua
       To gather in some debts, my son Lucentio
       Made me acquainted with a weighty cause
       Of love between your daughter and himself:
       And, for the good report I hear of you
30   And for the love he beareth to your daughter
       And she to him, to stay him not too long,
       I am content, in a good father's care,
       To have him match'd; and if you please to like
       No worse than I, upon some agreement
35   Me shall you find ready and willing
       With one consent to have her so bestow'd;
       For curious I cannot be with you,
       Signior Baptista, of whom I hear so well.

     BAP: Sir, pardon me in what I have to say:
40   Your plainness and your shortness please me well.
       Right true it is, your son Lucentio here
       Doth love my daughter and she loveth him,
       Or both dissemble deeply their affections:
       And therefore, if you say no more than this,
45   That like a father you will deal with him
       And pass my daughter a sufficient dower,
       The match is made, and all is done:
       Your son shall have my daughter with consent.

     TRA: I thank you, sir. Where then do you know best
50   We be affied and such assurance ta'en
       As shall with either part's agreement stand?

     BAP: Not in my house, Lucentio; for, you know,

Signior Baptista, we are happy to see you.
[To the Teacher]
Sir, this is the gentleman I told you about. I ask you to be a good father to me now; give me Bianca for my inheritance.

TEACHER: *Quiet, son! Sir, with your permission. Since I have come to Padua to gather in some debts, my son Lucentio has acquainted me with the serious matter of love between your daughter and himself. For the good report I hear about you, and for the love he bears to your daughter and she to him, do not keep him from this for too long. I am content, with the care of a good father, to have him matched. And if you are pleased, like I am, with some agreement that we make, you will find me ready and willing to have her married with my consent. I cannot be too demanding with you, Signior Baptista, because I hear so many great things about you.*

BAPTISTA: *Sir, pardon me in what I have to say. Your plainness and your shortness pleases me well. It is very true, your son Lucentio here loves my daughter and she loves him, or both are deeply pretending their affections. Therefore, if you say no more than this: you will deal with him like a father and pass my daughter a sufficient inheritance, then the match is made, and all is done. Your son shall have my daughter with my consent.*

TRANIO: *I thank you, sir. Do you know where, then, we may be formally engaged and provide such guarantees that will be agreeable to either party?*

BAPTISTA: *Not in my house, Lucentio, for you know, pitchers have ears, and*

Pitchers have ears, and I have many servants:
Besides, old Gremio is hearkening still;
55   And happily we might be interrupted.

Tra: Then at my lodging, an it like you:
There doth my father lie; and there, this night,
We'll pass the business privately and well.
Send for your daughter by your servant here:
60   My boy shall fetch the scrivener presently.
The worst is this, that, at so slender warning,
You are like to have a thin and slender pittance.

Bap: It likes me well. Cambio, hie you home,
And bid Bianca make her ready straight;
65   And, if you will, tell what hath happened,
Lucentio's father is arrived in Padua,
And how she's like to be Lucentio's wife.

Bio: I pray the gods she may with all my heart!

Tra: Dally not with the gods, but get thee gone.
                                        [Exit Biondello]
70   Signior Baptista, shall I lead the way?
Welcome! one mess is like to be your cheer:
Come, sir; we will better it in Pisa.

Bap: I follow you.   *[Exeunt Tranio, Pedant, and Baptista]*

[Re-enter Biondello]

Bio: Cambio!

75 Luc: What sayest thou, Biondello?

Bio: You saw my master wink and laugh upon you?

Luc: Biondello, what of that?

I have many servants. Besides, old Gremio is constantly watching and perhaps we might be interrupted.

TRANIO: Then at my lodging, if you like. My father stays there, and tonight, we'll conduct this business privately and well. Send your servant here to get your daughter. [Points to LUCENTIO as CAMBIO and winks at him] My servant will fetch the notary to draw up the contracts as soon as possible. The worst that could happen is that on such short notice, you are likely to have a thin and slender portion of food.

BAPTISTA: That suits me fine. Cambio, go straight home and tell Bianca to get ready right away. If you will, tell her what has happened: Lucentio's father has arrived in Padua, and she is likely to be Lucentio's wife.
[Lucentio as Cambio exits]

BIONDELLO: I pray to the gods she may, with all my heart!

TRANIO: Don't delay with the gods, but get going.   [Biondello exits]
Signior Baptista, should I lead the way? Welcome! One dish is likely to be your food and drink. Come, sir, we will make it better in Pisa.

BAPTISTA: I follow you.   [Tranio, Teacher, and Baptista exit]

[Biondello re-enters. Lucentio re-enters]

BIONDELLO: Cambio!

LUCENTIO: What do you say, Biondello?

BIONDELLO: You saw my master wink and laugh at you?

LUCENTIO: Biondello, so what?

BIO: Faith, nothing; but has left me here behind, to expound the
       meaning or moral of his signs and tokens.

80 LUC: I pray thee, moralize them.

BIO: Then thus. Baptista is safe, talking with the deceiving father
       of a deceitful son.

LUC: And what of him?

BIO: His daughter is to be brought by you to the supper.

85 LUC: And then?

BIO: The old priest of Saint Luke's church is at your command at
       all hours.

LUC: And what of all this?

BIO: I cannot tell; except they are busied about a counterfeit
90   assurance: take you assurance of her, 'cum privilegio ad
       imprimendum solum:' to the church; take the priest, clerk,
       and some sufficient honest witnesses:
       If this be not that you look for, I have no more to say,
       But bid Bianca farewell for ever and a day.

95 LUC: Hearest thou, Biondello?

BIO: I cannot tarry: I knew a wench married in an afternoon as
       she went to the garden for parsley to stuff a rabbit; and so
       may you, sir: and so, adieu, sir. My master hath appointed me
       to go to Saint Luke's, to bid the priest be ready to come
100   against you come with your appendix.   *[Exit]*

LUC: I may, and will, if she be so contented:
       She will be pleased; then wherefore should I doubt?
       Hap what hap may, I'll roundly go about her:
       It shall go hard if Cambio go without her.   *[Exit]*

172

BIONDELLO: *I swear, nothing. But he has left me here behind to tell you the meaning or moral of his signs and tokens.*

LUCENTIO: *I beg of you, moralize them.*

BIONDELLO: *Then listen to this: Baptista is safe, talking with the deceiving father of a deceitful son.*

LUCENTIO: *What about him?*

BIONDELLO: *His daughter is to be brought by you to the supper.*

LUCENTIO: *And then?*

BIONDELLO: *The old priest of Saint Luke's church is at your command at all hours.*

LUCENTIO: *What about all this?*

BIONDELLO: *I cannot tell, except they are keeping busy about a counterfeit guarantee. You are as assured of marrying her as a publisher who has the only rights to a book, or as they say, "cum privilegio ad imprimendum solum." Take the priest, clerk, and some sufficient honest witnesses to the church. If this isn't what you are looking for, I have no more to say, but bid Bianca farewell forever and a day.*

LUCENTIO: *Is this what you heard, Biondello?*

BIONDELLO: *I cannot stay long. I knew a wench married in an afternoon as she went to the garden for parsley to stuff a rabbit. So may you, sir. And so, adieu, sir. My master has appointed me to go to Saint Luke's to ask the priest to be ready when you come with your bride.*

[Biondello exits]

LUCENTIO: *I may, and I will, if she is pleased with this. She will be pleased. Then why should I doubt? Whatever happens, I'll be straightforward with her about this. She'll have to put up a strong fight to get Cambio to go without her.*   [Lucentio exits]

Scene 5
A public road.

[Enter Petruchio, Katherine, Hortensio, and Servants]

PET: Come on, i' God's name; once more toward our father's.
　　　Good Lord, how bright and goodly shines the moon!

KAT: The moon! the sun: it is not moonlight now.

PET: I say it is the moon that shines so bright.

5　　KAT: I know it is the sun that shines so bright.

PET: Now, by my mother's son, and that's myself,
　　　It shall be moon, or star, or what I list,
　　　Or ere I journey to your father's house.
　　　Go on, and fetch our horses back again.
10　　Evermore cross'd and cross'd; nothing but cross'd!

HOR: Say as he says, or we shall never go.

KAT: Forward, I pray, since we have come so far,
　　　And be it moon, or sun, or what you please:
　　　An if you please to call it a rush-candle,
15　　Henceforth I vow it shall be so for me.

PET: I say it is the moon.

KAT: I know it is the moon.

PET: Nay, then you lie: it is the blessed sun.

KAT: Then, God be bless'd, it is the blessed sun:
20　　But sun it is not, when you say it is not;
　　　And the moon changes even as your mind.
　　　What you will have it named, even that it is;
　　　And so it shall be so for Katherine.

174

Scene 5
A public road.

[Petruchio, Katherine, Hortensio, and Servants enter]

PETRUCHIO: *Come on, in God's name. Once more we go toward our father's. Good Lord, how bright and beautifully the moon shines!*

KATHERINE: *The moon? The sun! It is not moonlight now.*

PETRUCHIO: *I say it is the moon that shines so bright.*

KATHERINE: *I know it is the sun that shines so bright.*

PETRUCHIO: *Now, by my mother's son, and that's myself, it will be a moon, or a star, or whatever I choose, before I continue the journey to your father's house. Go on, and bring our horses back again. I am forever crossed and crossed, nothing but crossed!*

HORTENSIO: [To Katherine] *Say what he says, or we will never go.*

KATHERINE: *Forward, I beg you, since we have come so far; it can be moon, or sun, or whatever you please. If it pleases you to call it a cheap candle, from here on in, I vow it will be the same for me.*

PETRUCHIO: *I say it is the moon.*

KATHERINE: *I know it is the moon.*

PETRUCHIO: *No, then you lie. It is the blessed sun.*

KATHERINE: *Then, God be blessed, it is the blessed sun. But sun it is not when you say it is not and the moon changes even as your mind does. What you will name it, that it is, and so it will be for Katherine.*

HOR: Petruchio, go thy ways; the field is won.

25 PET: Well, forward, forward! thus the bowl should run,
And not unluckily against the bias.
But, soft! company is coming here.

[Enter Vincentio]
[To Vincentio]
Good morrow, gentle mistress: where away?
Tell me, sweet Kate, and tell me truly too,
30 Hast thou beheld a fresher gentlewoman?
Such war of white and red within her cheeks!
What stars do spangle heaven with such beauty,
As those two eyes become that heavenly face?
Fair lovely maid, once more good day to thee.
35 Sweet Kate, embrace her for her beauty's sake.

HOR: A' will make the man mad, to make a woman of him.

KAT: Young budding virgin, fair and fresh and sweet,
Whither away, or where is thy abode?
Happy the parents of so fair a child;
40 Happier the man, whom favourable stars
Allot thee for his lovely bed-fellow!

PET: Why, how now, Kate! I hope thou art not mad:
This is a man, old, wrinkled, faded, wither'd,
And not a maiden, as thou say'st he is.

45 KAT: Pardon, old father, my mistaking eyes,
That have been so bedazzled with the sun
That everything I look on seemeth green:
Now I perceive thou art a reverend father;
Pardon, I pray thee, for my mad mistaking.

50 PET: Do, good old grandsire; and withal make known
Which way thou travellest: if along with us,
We shall be joyful of thy company.

HORTENSIO: *Petruchio, give up, you have won.*

PETRUCHIO: *Well, forward, forward! This is the way a wife should act. But, quiet! We have company coming here.*

[Vincentio enters]
   [To Vincentio] *Good morning, gentle mistress, where are you going? Tell me, sweet Kate, truly, have you ever beheld a more radiant gentle- woman? Her cheeks are so red they are at war with her white skin! What stars light up heaven with such beauty as those two eyes that make that heavenly face so beautiful? Fair lovely maid, once more good day to you. Sweet Kate, embrace her because she is so beautiful.*

HORTENSIO: [Aside] *He will make the man mad, to make a woman of him.*

KATHERINE: [To Vincentio] *Young budding virgin, fair and fresh and sweet, where are you going; where do you live? The parents of so fair a child are happy, but happier will be the man whose good fortune it will be to have you for his lovely bedfellow!*

PETRUCHIO: *Why, what's going on, Kate? I hope you are not mad. This is a man, old, wrinkled, faded, withered, and not a maiden, as you say he is.*

KATHERINE: *Pardon, old father, my eyes make mistakes. They have been so dazzled by the sun that everything I look on seems to be green. Now I see you are a respected father. Pardon me, I beg of you, for my error.*

PETRUCHIO: *Do, good old grandfather. Let all of us know which way you travel. If you go along with us, we will be joyful for your company.*

177

VIN: Fair sir, and you my merry mistress,
    That with your strange encounter much amazed me,
55   My name is call'd Vincentio; my dwelling Pisa;
    And bound I am to Padua; there to visit
    A son of mine, which long I have not seen.

PET: What is his name?

VIN: Lucentio, gentle sir.

60 PET: Happily met; the happier for thy son.
    And now by law, as well as reverend age,
    I may entitle thee my loving father:
    The sister to my wife, this gentlewoman,
    Thy son by this hath married. Wonder not,
65   Nor be grieved: she is of good esteem,
    Her dowry wealthy, and of worthy birth;
    Beside, so qualified as may beseem
    The spouse of any noble gentleman.
    Let me embrace with old Vincentio,
70   And wander we to see thy honest son,
    Who will of thy arrival be full joyous.

VIN: But is it true? or else is it your pleasure,
    Like pleasant travellers, to break a jest
    Upon the company you overtake?

75 HOR: I do assure thee, father, so it is.

PET: Come, go along, and see the truth hereof;
    For our first merriment hath made thee jealous.
                      [Exeunt all but Hortensio]

HOR: Well, Petruchio, this has put me in heart.
    Have to my widow! and if she be froward,
80   Then hast thou taught Hortensio to be untoward.

                                   [Exit]

VINCENTIO: *Fair sir, and you, my merry mistress who much amazed me with your strange encounter, my name is Vincentio, my dwelling Pisa, and I am going to Padua to visit a son of mine whom I have not seen for a long time.*

PETRUCHIO: *What is his name?*

VINCENTIO: *Lucentio, gentle sir.*

PETRUCHIO: *It is a good thing that we met, and better for your son. Now by law, as well as by your old age, I may call you my loving father. Your son has married the sister to my wife, this gentlewoman. Don't wonder or be grieved. She has a good reputation, her dowry is wealthy, and she is of worthy birth. She also has many other qualities that are appropriate for the spouse of any noble gentleman. Let me hug you, old Vincentio, and we will wander to see your honest son, who will be filled with joy over your arrival.*

VINCENTIO: *But is this true, or is it your pleasure, like merry travelers, to make fun of the company that you meet on the way?*

HORTENSIO: *I assure you, father, it is true.*

PETRUCHIO: *Come, go along, and see the truth of what we say, because the first joke we played on you has made you suspicious.*

[All exit but Hortensio]

HORTENSIO: *Well, Petruchio, this has put me in good spirits. Here I come, my widow! And if she is disobedient, then you have taught Hortensio how to be firm.*

[Hortensio exits]

ACT V

SCENE 1
Padua. Before Lucentio's house.

[Gremio discovered. Enter behind Biondello, Lucentio, and Bianca]

BIO: Softly and swiftly, sir; for the priest is ready.

LUC: I fly, Biondello: but they may chance to need thee at home;
therefore leave us.

BIO: Nay, faith, I'll see the church o' your back; and then come
5   back to my master's as soon as I can.
                    [Exeunt Lucentio, Bianca, and Biondello]

GRE: I marvel Cambio comes not all this while.

[Enter Petruchio, Katherine, Vincentio, Grumio, with Attendants]

PET: Sir, here's the door, this is Lucentio's house:
My father's bears more toward the market-place;
Thither must I, and here I leave you, sir.

10   VIN: You shall not choose but drink before you go:
I think I shall command your welcome here,
And, by all likelihood, some cheer is toward.   *[Knocks]*

GRE: They're busy within; you were best knock
louder.

ACT V

SCENE 1
Padua. Before Lucentio's house.

[Gremio is already onstage. Biondello, Lucentio, and Bianca enter]

BIONDELLO: *Quietly and swiftly, sir, for the priest is ready.*

LUCENTIO: *I fly, Biondello. But they might need you at home. Therefore, leave us.*

BIONDELLO: *No. I'll see the church at your back and then come back to my master's as soon as I can.*

[Lucentio, Bianca, and Biondello exit]

GREMIO: *I marvel that Cambio doesn't come during all this.*

[Petruchio, Katherine, Vincentio, Grumio, and Attendants enter]

PETRUCHIO: *Sir, here's the door, this is Lucentio's house. My father's house is closer to the market-place. There I must go, and here I leave you, sir.*

VINCENTIO: *You have no choice but to have a drink before you go. I think I shall announce your welcome here, and, by all likelihood, we'll have some food and drink.* [Knocks]

GREMIO: *They're busy within; you better knock louder.*

[Pedant looks out of the window]

15 PED: What's he that knocks as he would beat down the gate?

VIN: Is Signior Lucentio within, sir?

PED: He's within, sir, but not to be spoken withal.

VIN: What if a man bring him a hundred pound or two, to make merry withal?

20 PED: Keep your hundred pounds to yourself: he shall need none, so long as I live.

PET: Nay, I told you your son was well beloved in Padua.   Do you hear, sir? To leave frivolous circumstances, I pray you, tell Signior Lucentio that his father is come from Pisa, and is
25   here at the door to speak with him.

PED: Thou liest: his father is come from Padua and here looking out at the window.

VIN: Art thou his father?

PED: Ay, sir; so his mother says, if I may believe her.

30 PET: *[To Vincentio]* Why, how now, gentleman! why, this is flat knavery, to take upon you another man's name.

PED: Lay hands on the villain: I believe a' means to cozen somebody in this city under my countenance.

[Re-enter Biondello]

BIO: I have seen them in the church together:
35   God send 'em good shipping! But who is here? mine old master Vincentio! now we are undone and brought to nothing.

[The Teacher looks out of the window]

TEACHER: *Who is it that knocks as if he would beat down the gate?*

VINCENTIO: *Is Signior Lucentio within, sir?*

TEACHER: *He's within, sir, but not to be spoken with.*

VINCENTIO: *What if a man brings him a hundred pound or two, to make merry with?*

TEACHER: *Keep your hundred pounds to yourself. He won't need it, as long as I live.*

PETRUCHIO: *Nay, I told you your son was well loved in Padua. Do you hear, sir? Leaving out unnecessary details, I beg you, tell Signior Lucentio that his father has come from Pisa, and is here at the door to speak with him.*

TEACHER: *You lie. His father has come from Padua and yet is here looking out at the window.*

VINCENTIO: *Are you his father?*

TEACHER: *Yes, sir. That's what his mother says, if I can believe her.*

PETRUCHIO: [To Vincentio] *Why, what's going on, gentleman? This is complete trickery, to take another man's name as your own.*

TEACHER: *Grab the villain! I believe he means to cheat somebody in this city while pretending to be me.*

[Re-enter Biondello]

BIONDELLO: *I have seen them in the church together. God send them good luck! But who is here? My old master, Vincentio! Now we are ruined and have nothing.*

VIN: *[Seeing Biondello]* Come hither, crack-hemp.

BIO: I hope I may choose, sir.

VIN: Come hither, you rogue. What, have you forgot me?

40 BIO: Forgot you! no, sir: I could not forget you, for I never saw you before in all my life.

VIN: What, you notorious villain, didst thou never see thy master's father, Vincentio?

BIO: What, my old worshipful old master? yes, marry, sir: see
45 where he looks out of the window.

VIN: Is't so, indeed? *[Beats Biondello]*

BIO: Help, help, help! here's a madman will murder me.
[Exit]

PED: Help, son! help, Signior Baptista! *[Exit from above]*

50 PET: Prithee, Kate, let's stand aside and see the end of this controversy. *[They retire]*

[Re-enter Pedant below; Tranio, Baptista, and Servants]

TRA: Sir, what are you that offer to beat my servant?

VIN: What am I, sir! nay, what are you, sir? O immortal gods! O
fine villain! A silken doublet! a velvet hose! a scarlet cloak!
55 and a copatain hat! O, I am undone! I am undone! while I
play the good husband at home, my son and my servant
spend all at the university.

TRA: How now! what's the matter?

BAP: What, is the man lunatic?

VINCENTIO: [Seeing Biondello] *Come here; you are suitable for hanging.*

BIONDELLO: *I hope I may choose, sir.*

VINCENTIO: *Come here, you rogue. Have you forgotten me?*

BIONDELLO: *Forgotten you! No, sir. I could not forget you, because I never saw you before in all my life.*

VINCENTIO: *What, you notorious villain, you never saw your master's father, Vincentio?*

BIONDELLO: *My worshipful old master? Yes, indeed, sir. See where he looks out of the window.*

VINCENTIO: *Is it so, indeed?* [Beats Biondello]

BIONDELLO: *Help, help, help! Here's a madman who will murder me.*
[Biondello exits]

TEACHER: *Help, son! Help, Signior Baptista!* [Exits from above]

PETRUCHIO: *I ask you, Kate, let's stand aside and see the end of this controversy.* [They stand aside]

[Re-enter the Teacher below with Tranio, Baptista, and Servants]

TRANIO: *Sir, what kind of man are you that you offer to beat my servant?*

VINCENTIO: *What am I, sir! No, what are you, sir? Oh, immortal gods! Oh, finely dressed villain! A silken shirt! Velvet stockings! A scarlet cloak! And a high-crowned hat! Oh, I am ruined! I am undone! While I play the good husband at home, my son and my servant spend all my money at the university.*

TRANIO: *What's going on? What's the matter?*

BAPTISTA: *Is the man a lunatic?*

60   TRA: Sir, you seem a sober ancient gentleman by your habit, but
            your words show you a madman. Why, sir, what 'cerns it you
            if I wear pearl and gold? I thank my good father, I am able to
            maintain it.

     VIN: Thy father! O villain! he is a sailmaker in Bergamo.

65   BAP: You mistake, sir, you mistake, sir. Pray, what do you think is
            his name?

     VIN: His name! as if I knew not his name: I have brought him up
            ever since he was three years old, and his name is Tranio.

     PED: Away, away, mad ass! his name is Lucentio and he is mine
70   only son, and heir to the lands of me, Signior Vincentio.

     VIN: Lucentio! O, he hath murdered his master!
            Lay hold on him, I charge you, in the duke's name. O, my
            son, my son! Tell me, thou villain, where is my son Lucentio?

     TRA: Call forth an officer.

     [Enter one with an Officer]
75   Carry this mad knave to the gaol. Father Baptista, I charge
            you see that he be forthcoming.

     VIN: Carry me to the gaol!

     GRE: Stay, officer: he shall not go to prison.

     BAP: Talk not, Signior Gremio: I say he shall go to prison.

80   GRE: Take heed, Signior Baptista, lest you be cony-catched in this
            business: I dare swear this is the right Vincentio.

     PED: Swear, if thou darest.

     GRE: Nay, I dare not swear it.

186

TRANIO: *Sir, you seem like a sober old gentleman by your clothing, but your words show that you are a madman. Sir, what concern is it to you if I wear pearl and gold? I thank my good father that I am able to afford it.*

VINCENTIO: *Your father! Oh, villain! He is a sailmaker in Bergamo.*

BAPTISTA: *You are mistaken, sir. Tell me, what do you think his name is?*

VINCENTIO: *His name! As if I didn't know his name. I have brought him up ever since he was three years old, and his name is Tranio.*

TEACHER: *Away, away, mad ass! His name is Lucentio; he is my only son, and heir to my lands, Signior Vincentio.*

VINCENTIO: *Lucentio! Oh, he has murdered his master! Grab hold of him, I command you, in the duke's name. Oh, my son, my son! Tell me, you villain, where is my son Lucentio?*

TRANIO: *Call for an officer.*

[A servant enters with an Officer]
Carry this mad knave to the jail. Father Baptista, I order you to see that he is produced.

VINCENTIO: *Carry me to the jail!*

GREMIO: *Wait, officer, he will not go to prison.*

BAPTISTA: *Do not talk, Signior Gremio. I say he will go to prison.*

GREMIO: *Take heed, Signior Baptista, or else you'll be cheated in this business. I swear that this is the right Vincentio.*

TEACHER: *Swear, if you dare.*

GREMIO: *No, I dare not swear it.*

TRA: Then thou wert best say that I am not Lucentio.

85 GRE: Yes, I know thee to be Signior Lucentio.

BAP: Away with the dotard! to the gaol with him!

VIN: Thus strangers may be hailed and abused:
     O monstrous villain!

[Re-enter Biondello, with Lucentio and Bianca]

BIO: O! we are spoiled and—yonder he is: deny him, forswear
90   him, or else we are all undone.

LUC: *[Kneeling]* Pardon, sweet father.

VIN: Lives my sweet son?
     [Exeunt Biondello, Tranio, and Pedant, as fast as may be]

BIA: Pardon, dear father.

BAP: How hast thou offended?
95   Where is Lucentio?

LUC: Here's Lucentio,
     Right son to the right Vincentio;
     That have by marriage made thy daughter mine,
     While counterfeit supposes bleared thine eyne.

100 GRE: Here's packing, with a witness to deceive us all!

VIN: Where is that damned villain Tranio,
     That faced and braved me in this matter so?

BAP: Why, tell me, is not this my Cambio?

BIA: Cambio is changed into Lucentio.

TRANIO: *Then you might as well say that I am not Lucentio.*

GREMIO: *Yes, I know you to be Signior Lucentio.*

BAPTISTA: *Away with the foolish old man! To the jail with him!*

VINCENTIO: *Just like that, strangers are bothered and abused. Oh, monstrous villain!*

[Re-enter Biondello, with Lucentio and Bianca]

BIONDELLO: *Oh! We are ruined and—he is over there. Deny him, refuse him, or else we are all undone.*

LUCENTIO: [Kneeling] *Pardon me, sweet father.*

VINCENTIO: *Does my sweet son live?*
　　　　　　　[Biondello, Tranio, and Teacher, exit as fast as they can]

BIANCA: *Pardon me, dear father.*

BAPTISTA: *How have you offended them? Where is Lucentio?*

LUCENTIO: *Here's Lucentio, the right son to the right Vincentio, who has by marriage made your daughter mine, while false impersonators blurred your eyes.*

GREMIO: *Here's plotting, with a vengeance, to deceive us all!*

VINCENTIO: *Where is that damned villain Tranio, that defied me so in this matter?*

BAPTISTA: *Why, tell me, is this not my Cambio?*

BIANCA:　*Cambio is changed into Lucentio.*

105 LUC: Love wrought these miracles. Bianca's love
            Made me exchange my state with Tranio,
            While he did bear my countenance in the town;
            And happily I have arrived at the last
            Unto the wished haven of my bliss.
110   What Tranio did, myself enforced him to;
            Then pardon him, sweet father, for my sake.

    VIN: I'll slit the villain's nose, that would have sent me to the
            gaol.

    BAP: But do you hear, sir? have you married my daughter with-
115   out asking my good will?

    VIN: Fear not, Baptista; we will content you, go to: but I will in,
            to be revenged for this villainy.   [Exit]

    BAP: And I, to sound the depth of this knavery.   [Exit]

    LUC: Look not pale, Bianca; thy father will not frown.
                            [Exeunt Lucentio and Bianca]

120 GRE: My cake is dough; but I'll in among the rest,
            Out of hope of all, but my share of the feast.   [Exit]

    KAT: Husband, let's follow, to see the end of this ado.

    PET: First kiss me, Kate, and we will.

    KAT: What, in the midst of the street?

125 PET: What, art thou ashamed of me?

    KAT: No, sir, God forbid; but ashamed to kiss.

    PET: Why, then let's home again. Come, sirrah, let's away.

LUCENTIO: *Love caused these miracles. Bianca's love made me change my place with Tranio, while he pretended to be me in town. Happily I have at last arrived at the wished-for haven of my bliss. What Tranio did, I forced him to. Pardon him, sweet father, for my sake.*

VINCENTIO: *I'll slit the villain's nose, he who would have sent me to the jail.*

BAPTISTA: *But do you hear, sir; have you married my daughter without asking my good will?*

VINCENTIO: *Fear not, Baptista, we will make you content. Give it up! But I will go in to be avenged for this villainy.*   [Vincentio exits]

BAPTISTA: *And I will too, to find out the depth of this falseness.*
                                                       [Baptista: exits]

LUCENTIO: *Don't look pale, Bianca; your father will not frown.*
                                          [Lucentio and Bianca exit]

GREMIO: *I've failed, but I'll go in among the rest. I'm out of hope for everything except my share of the feast.*   [Gremio exits]

KATHERINE: *Husband, let's follow, to see the end of this fuss.*

PETRUCHIO: *First kiss me, Kate, and we will.*

KATHERINE: *What, in the middle of the street?*

PETRUCHIO: *What, are you ashamed of me?*

KATHERINE: *No, sir, God forbid, but I'm ashamed to kiss.*

PETRUCHIO: *Why, then let's go home again. Come, young fellow, let's go away.*

KAT: Nay, I will give thee a kiss: now pray thee, love, stay.

PET: Is not this well? Come, my sweet Kate:
130   Better once than never, for never too late.

[Exeunt]

Scene 2
Padua. Lucentio's house.

[Enter Baptista, Vincentio, Gremio, the Pedant, Lucentio, Bianca, Petruchio, Katherine, Hortensio, and Widow, Tranio, Biondello, and Grumio. The Serving-men with Tranio bring in a banquet]

LUC: At last, though long, our jarring notes agree:
        And time it is, when raging war is done,
        To smile at scapes and perils overblown.
        My fair Bianca, bid my father welcome,
5   While I with self-same kindness welcome thine.
        Brother Petruchio, sister Katherine,
        And thou, Hortensio, with thy loving widow,
        Feast with the best, and welcome to my house:
        My banquet is to close our stomachs up,
10   After our great good cheer. Pray you, sit down;
        For now we sit to chat as well as eat.

PET: Nothing but sit and sit, and eat and eat!

BAP: Padua affords this kindness, son Petruchio.

PET: Padua affords nothing but what is kind.

15   HOR: For both our sakes, I would that word were true.

PET: Now, for my life, Hortensio fears his widow.

KATHERINE: *No, I will give you a kiss.* [She does] *Now I beg you, love, stay.*

PETRUCHIO: *Is this not a good thing? Come, my sweet Kate, better once than never, for never is too late.*

[They exit]

Scene 2
Padua. Lucentio's house.

[Enter Baptista, Vincentio, Gremio, the Teacher, Lucentio, Bianca, Petruchio, Katherine, Hortensio, and Widow, Tranio, Biondello, and Grumio. The Servants, with Tranio, bring in a banquet]

LUCENTIO: *At last, though it was long, our ill-sounding notes agree. It is time, when raging war is done, to smile at escapes and perils that are now past. My fair Bianca, welcome my father, while I, with the exact same kindness, welcome yours. Brother Petruchio, sister Katherine, and you, Hortensio, with your loving widow, feast with the best, and welcome to my house. My banquet is to provide the finale to our feast, after our great, good cheer. Please, all of you, sit down, for now we sit to chat as well as eat.*

PETRUCHIO: *Nothing but sit and sit, and eat and eat!*

BAPTISTA: *Padua affords this kindness, son Petruchio.*

PETRUCHIO: *Padua affords nothing but what is kind.*

HORTENSIO: *For both of our sakes, I wish what you said was true.*

PETRUCHIO: *Now, by my life, Hortensio fears his widow.*

WID: Then never trust me, if I be afeard.

PET: You are very sensible, and yet you miss my sense:
     I mean, Hortensio is afeard of you.

20 WID: He that is giddy thinks the world turns round.

PET: Roundly replied.

KAT: Mistress, how mean you that?

WID: Thus I conceive by him.

PET: Conceives by me! How likes Hortensio that?

25 HOR: My widow says, thus she conceives her tale.

PET: Very well mended. Kiss him for that, good widow.

KAT: 'He that is giddy thinks the world turns round:'
     I pray you, tell me what you meant by that.

WID: Your husband, being troubled with a shrew,
30   Measures my husband's sorrow by his woe:
     And now you know my meaning.

KAT: A very mean meaning.

WID: Right, I mean you.

KAT: And I am mean indeed, respecting you.

35 PET: To her, Kate!

HOR: To her, widow!

PET: A hundred marks, my Kate does put her down.

WIDOW: Then never trust me, if I am afraid.

PETRUCHIO: You are very sensible, and yet you miss my sense. I mean, Hortensio is afraid of you.

WIDOW: He that is dizzy thinks it is the world that turns around.

PETRUCHIO: Well said.

KATHERINE: Mistress, what do you mean by that?

WIDOW: I conceive of this by watching him.

PETRUCHIO: Conceives by me! How does Hortensio like that?

HORTENSIO: My widow says this is how she conceives her tale.

PETRUCHIO: Very well mended. Kiss him for that, good widow.

KATHERINE: "He that is dizzy thinks it is the world that turns around." Please, tell me what you meant by that.

WIDOW: Your husband, troubled with a shrew, measures my husband's sorrow by his own woe. Now you know my meaning.

KATHERINE: A very nasty meaning.

WIDOW: Right. I mean you.

KATHERINE: And I am mean, indeed, when it comes to you.

PETRUCHIO: To her, Kate!

HORTENSIO: To her, widow!

PETRUCHIO: I bet a hundred dollars, that my Kate puts her down.

HOR: That's my office.

PET: Spoke like an officer; ha' to thee, lad!
                              [Drinks to Hortensio]

40 BAP: How likes Gremio these quick-witted folks?

GRE: Believe me, sir, they butt together well.

BIA: Head, and butt! an hasty-witted body
      Would say your head and butt were head and horn.

VIN: Ay, mistress bride, hath that awaken'd you?

45 BIA: Ay, but not frighted me; therefore I'll sleep again.

PET: Nay, that you shall not: since you have begun,
      Have at you for a bitter jest or two!

BIA: Am I your bird? I mean to shift my bush;
      And then pursue me as you draw your bow.
50   You are welcome all.
                    [Exeunt Bianca, Katherine, and Widow]

PET: She hath prevented me. Here, Signior Tranio.
      This bird you aim'd at, though you hit her not;
      Therefore a health to all that shot and miss'd.

TRA: O, sir, Lucentio slipp'd me like his greyhound,
55   Which runs himself and catches for his master.

PET: A good swift simile, but something currish.

TRA: 'Tis well, sir, that you hunted for yourself:
      'Tis thought your deer does hold you at a bay.

BAP: O ho, Petruchio! Tranio hits you now.

196

HORTENSIO: *That's my duty.*

PETRUCHIO: *Spoken like an officer. Here's to you, lad!*
[Drinks to Hortensio]

BAPTISTA: *How does Gremio like these quick-witted folks?*

GREMIO: *Believe me, sir, they butt heads together well.*

BIANCA: *Head, and butt! A quick-witted person would say your head and butt were a head with a cuckold's horn.*

VINCENTIO: *Mistress bride, has this awakened you?*

BIANCA: *Yes, but not frightened me. Therefore I'll sleep again.*

PETRUCHIO: *No, that you will not. Since you have begun, I'm going to have at you for a sharp jest or two!*

BIANCA: *Am I your hunted bird? I mean to shift to a different bush. Then you pursue me like an archer who draws his bow. You are all welcome.*
[Bianca, Katherine, and Widow exit]

PETRUCHIO: *She has escaped me. Here, Signior Tranio. This bird you aimed at, even though you did not hit her. Therefore, let's drink to all who shot and missed.*

TRANIO: *Oh, sir, Lucentio let me loose like his greyhound, which runs himself and catches for his master.*

PETRUCHIO: *A good swift simile, but somewhat dog-like.*

TRANIO: *It is well, sir, that you hunted for yourself. It is thought your deer holds you off like baying dogs.*

BAPTISTA: *Oh, ho, Petruchio! Tranio hits you now.*

60   Luc: I thank thee for that gird, good Tranio.

       Hor: Confess, confess, hath he not hit you here?

       Pet: A' has a little gall'd me, I confess;
           And, as the jest did glance away from me,
           'Tis ten to one it maim'd you two outright.

65   Bap: Now, in good sadness, son Petruchio,
           I think thou hast the veriest shrew of all.

       Pet: Well, I say no: and therefore for assurance
           Let's each one send unto his wife;
           And he whose wife is most obedient
70   To come at first when he doth send for her,
           Shall win the wager which we will propose.

       Hor: Content. What is the wager?

       Luc: Twenty crowns.

       Pet: Twenty crowns!
75   I'll venture so much of my hawk or hound,
           But twenty times so much upon my wife.

       Luc: A hundred then.

       Hor: Content.

       Pet: A match! 'tis done.

80   Hor: Who shall begin?

       Luc: That will I.
           Go, Biondello, bid your mistress come to me.

       Bio: I go.   *[Exit]*

LUCENTIO: *I thank you for that sharp remark, good Tranio.*

HORTENSIO: *Confess, confess. Hasn't he hit on that one?*

PETRUCHIO: *He has scratched me a little, I confess. And, because the jest missed me, it is ten to one it maimed you two outright.*

BAPTISTA: *Now, in good sadness, son Petruchio, I think you have the most shrewish one of all.*

PETRUCHIO: *Well, I say no. Therefore, for assurance, let each of us send for his wife. He whose wife is most obedient and comes first when he sends for her will win the wager which we will propose.*

HORTENSIO: *Fine. What is the wager?*

LUCENTIO: *Twenty gold pieces.*

PETRUCHIO: *Twenty gold pieces! I'll bet so much on my hawk or hound, but twenty times as much upon my wife.*

LUCENTIO: *A hundred then.*

HORTENSIO: *Fine.*

PETRUCHIO: *A match! It is done.*

HORTENSIO: *Who will begin?*

LUCENTIO: *I will. Go, Biondello, ask your mistress to come to me.*

BIONDELLO: *I go.* [Biondello: exits]

BAP: Son, I'll be your half, Bianca comes.

85   LUC: I'll have no halves; I'll bear it all myself.

[Re-enter Biondello]
       How now! what news?

BIO: Sir, my mistress sends you word
       That she is busy and she cannot come.

PET: How! she is busy and she cannot come!
90   Is that an answer?

GRE: Ay, and a kind one too:
       Pray God, sir, your wife send you not a worse.

PET: I hope better.

HOR: Sirrah Biondello, go and entreat my wife
95   To come to me forthwith.   *[Exit Biondello]*

PET: O, ho! entreat her!
       Nay, then she must needs come.

HOR: I am afraid, sir,
       Do what you can, yours will not be entreated.

[Re-enter Biondello]
100   Now, where's my wife?

BIO: She says you have some goodly jest in hand:
       She will not come: she bids you come to her.

PET: Worse and worse; she will not come! O vile,
       Intolerable, not to be endured!
105   Sirrah Grumio, go to your mistress;
       Say, I command her to come to me.   *[Exit Grumio]*

BAPTISTA: *Son, I'll take half of that bet. Bianca comes.*

LUCENTIO: *I'll have no one taking half. I'll carry it all myself.*

[Re-enter Biondello]
   What's going on? What news?

BIONDELLO: *Sir, my mistress sends you word that she is busy and she cannot come.*

PETRUCHIO: *What? She is busy and she cannot come! Is that an answer?*

GREMIO: *Yes, and a kind one too. Pray God, sir, your wife doesn't send you a worse answer.*

PETRUCHIO: *I hope it's better.*

HORTENSIO: *Servant Biondello, go and entreat my wife to come to me right away.*   [Biondello exits]

PETRUCHIO: *Oh, ho! Entreat her! No, then she'll have to come.*

HORTENSIO: *I am afraid, sir, that do what you can, yours will not be entreated.*

[Re-enter Biondello]
   Now, where's my wife?

BIONDELLO: *She says you have some good joke in mind. She will not come. She asks you to come to her.*

PETRUCHIO: *Worse and worse, she will not come! Oh, it's vile, intolerable, and not to be endured! Servant Grumio, go to your mistress. Say that I command her to come to me.*   [Grumio exits]

HOR: I know her answer.

PET: What?

HOR: She will not.

110 PET: The fouler fortune mine, and there an end.

BAP: Now, by my holidame, here comes Katherine!

[Re-enter Katherine]

KAT: What is your will, sir, that you send for me?

PET: Where is your sister, and Hortensio's wife?

KAT: They sit conferring by the parlor fire.

115 PET: Go fetch them hither: if they deny to come,
Swinge me them soundly forth unto their husbands:
Away, I say, and bring them hither straight. *[Exit Katherine]*

LUC: Here is a wonder, if you talk of a wonder.

HOR: And so it is: I wonder what it bodes.

120 PET: Marry, peace it bodes, and love and quiet life,
And awful rule and right supremacy;
And, to be short, what not, that's sweet and happy?

BAP: Now, fair befal thee, good Petruchio!
The wager thou hast won; and I will add
125 Unto their losses twenty thousand crowns;
Another dowry to another daughter,
For she is changed, as she had never been.

PET: Nay, I will win my wager better yet
And show more sign of her obedience,

HORTENSIO: *I know what her answer will be.*

PETRUCHIO: *What?*

HORTENSIO: *She will not.*

PETRUCHIO: *Then I have bad luck, and that will be the end of it.*

BAPTISTA: *Now, by the Virgin Mary, here comes Katherine!*

[Re-enter Katherine]

KATHERINE: *What is your will, sir, that you sent for me?*

PETRUCHIO: *Where is your sister, and Hortensio's wife?*

KATHERINE: *They sit conferring by the parlor fire.*

PETRUCHIO: *Go fetch them here. If they refuse to come, beat them soundly for me and bring them to their husbands. Away, I say, and bring them directly here.*   [Katherine exits]

LUCENTIO: *Here is a wonder, if you talk of a wonder.*

HORTENSIO: *So it is. I wonder what it predicts.*

PETRUCHIO: *Indeed, it predicts peace and love and quiet life, and awe-filled rule and proper supremacy. To be short, everything that's sweet and happy.*

BAPTISTA: *Now, good fortune comes to you, good Petruchio! They have lost; I will add twenty thousand gold pieces, another dowry to another daughter, for she is changed, as she had never been before.*

PETRUCHIO: *No, I will win my wager yet and show you more signs of her*

130   Her new-built virtue and obedience.
         See where she comes and brings your froward wives
         As prisoners to her womanly persuasion.

[Re-enter Katherine, with Bianca and Widow]
         Katherine, that cap of yours becomes you not:
         Off with that bauble, throw it under-foot.

135 Wɪᴅ: Lord, let me never have a cause to sigh,
         Till I be brought to such a silly pass!

     Bɪᴀ: Fie! what a foolish duty call you this?

     Lᴜᴄ: I would your duty were as foolish too:
         The wisdom of your duty, fair Bianca,
140   Hath cost me an hundred crowns since supper-time.

     Bɪᴀ: The more fool you, for laying on my duty.

     Pᴇᴛ: Katherine, I charge thee, tell these headstrong women
         What duty they do owe their lords and husbands.

     Wɪᴅ: Come, come, you're mocking: we will have no telling.

145 Pᴇᴛ: Come on, I say; and first begin with her.

     Wɪᴅ: She shall not.

     Pᴇᴛ: I say she shall: and first begin with her.

     Kᴀᴛ: Fie, fie! unknit that threatening unkind brow,
         And dart not scornful glances from those eyes,
150   To wound thy lord, thy king, thy governor:
         It blots thy beauty as frosts do bite the meads,
         Confounds thy fame as whirlwinds shake fair buds,
         And in no sense is meet or amiable.
         A woman moved is like a fountain troubled,
155   Muddy, ill-seeming, thick, bereft of beauty;

obedience, her newly-built virtue and obedience. See how she comes and brings your stubborn wives like prisoners to her womanly persuasion.

[Re-enter Katherine, with Bianca and Widow]
Katherine, that cap of yours is not attractive on you. Take off that showy piece of junk; throw it underfoot.

WIDOW: *Lord, let me never have a reason to sigh, until I am brought to such a silly state as this!*

BIANCA: *For shame! What kind of foolish duty do you call this?*

LUCENTIO: *I wish your duty to me was just as foolish. The wisdom of your duty, fair Bianca, has cost me a hundred gold pieces since suppertime.*

BIANCA: *You are a fool, for betting on my duty.*

PETRUCHIO: *Katherine, I command you, tell these headstrong women what duty they owe to their lords and husbands.*

WIDOW: *Come, come, you're mocking. We will not be told what to do.*

PETRUCHIO: *Come on, I say, and first begin with her.*

WIDOW: *She will not.*

PETRUCHIO: *I say she will. And first begin with her.*

KATHERINE: *Shame, shame! Unknit that threatening unkind brow, and don't shoot scornful glances from those eyes, to wound your lord, your king, your governor. It makes a blot on your beauty like the frost that bites the meadows; it destroys your reputation as whirlwinds shake the fair buds of flowers; and it is in no sense right or friendly. A woman angered is like a troubled fountain, muddy, ugly, thick, lacking beauty; while it is this way, no one who is dry or thirsty will condescend to sip or touch one drop of it. Your husband is your lord, your life, your keeper, your head,*

And while it is so, none so dry or thirsty
Will deign to sip or touch one drop of it.
Thy husband is thy lord, thy life, thy keeper,
Thy head, thy sovereign; one that cares for thee,
160   And for thy maintenance commits his body
To painful labour both by sea and land,
To watch the night in storms, the day in cold,
Whilst thou liest warm at home, secure and safe;
And craves no other tribute at thy hands
165   But love, fair looks and true obedience;
Too little payment for so great a debt.
Such duty as the subject owes the prince
Even such a woman oweth to her husband;
And when she is froward, peevish, sullen, sour,
170   And not obedient to his honest will,
What is she but a foul contending rebel
And graceless traitor to her loving lord?
I am ashamed that women are so simple
To offer war where they should kneel for peace;
175   Or seek for rule, supremacy and sway,
When they are bound to serve, love and obey.
Why are our bodies soft and weak and smooth,
Unapt to toil and trouble in the world,
But that our soft conditions and our hearts
180   Should well agree with our external parts?
Come, come, you froward and unable worms!
My mind hath been as big as one of yours,
My heart as great, my reason haply more,
To bandy word for word and frown for frown;
185   But now I see our lances are but straws,
Our strength as weak, our weakness past compare,
That seeming to be most which we indeed least are.
Then vail your stomachs, for it is no boot,
And place your hands below your husband's foot:
190   In token of which duty, if he please,
My hand is ready; may it do him ease.

PET: Why, there's a wench! Come on, and kiss me, Kate.

your ruler, one that cares for you, and for your maintenance; he commits his body to painful labor, both by sea and land, to keep awake at night in storms, the day in cold, while you lie warm at home, secure, and safe. He craves no other tribute from your hands but love, fair looks, and true obedience–too little of a payment for so great a debt. The duty that the subject owes the prince is the same duty a woman owes her husband. When she is nasty, peevish, sullen, sour, and not obedient to his will, what is she but a foul war-like rebel and graceless traitor to her loving lord? I am ashamed that women are so foolish as to offer war when they should kneel for peace, or seek to rule or govern supreme, when they are bound to serve, love, and obey. Why are our bodies soft and weak and smooth, unfit to toil and trouble in the world, except that our soft conditions and our hearts should agree with our external parts? Come, come, you disobedient and weak worms! My mind is as self-important as yours, my courage as great, my reasoning more to toss words back and forth and frown for frown. But, now, I see our lances are only straws, our strength is weak, our weakness beyond comparison. What we have the most of, that is what we are least. Therefore, subdue your pride, for it is futile, and place your hands below your husband's foot, to show your duty. If my husband pleases, my hand is ready, if he so desires.

PETRUCHIO: Why, there's a wench! Come on, and kiss me, Kate.

LUC: Well, go thy ways, old lad; for thou shalt ha't.

VIN: 'Tis a good hearing when children are toward.

195 LUC: But a harsh hearing when women are froward.

PET: Come, Kate, we'll to bed.
We three are married, but you two are sped.
[To Lucentio]
'Twas I won the wager, though you hit the white;
And, being a winner, God give you good night!
[Exeunt Petruchio and Katherine]

200 HOR: Now, go thy ways; thou hast tamed a curst shrew.

LUC: 'Tis a wonder, by your leave, she will be tamed so.

[Exeunt]

LUCENTIO: *Well, go your ways, old lad, for you have won.*

VINCENTIO: *It is good to hear when children are obedient.*

LUCENTIO: *But harsh to hear when women are disobedient.*

PETRUCHIO: *Come, Kate, we'll go to bed. We three couples are married, but you two are done for.*
[To Lucentio]
It was I who won the bet, though you hit the white of the bullseye, and since I am a winner, God give you a good night!

[Petruchio and Katherine exit]

HORTENSIO: *Now, go your way, you have tamed a cursed shrew.*

LUCENTIO: *It is a wonder, if I may say so, that she has been tamed, too.*

[All exit]

Study Guide

Note that the older man who desires to wed Bianca is named Gremio. Grumio, however, is one of the servants in Petruchio's household.

INDUCTION, SCENE 1

1. Christopher Sly, a drunk tinker, is being scolded by the hostess of a bar. Why is she angry with him? What is his response?

2. What, according to the lord and his huntsmen, are the qualities of a good hunting dog?

3. The lord and his two huntsmen plan to play an elaborate practical joke on Christopher Sly. What are they going to do to him?

4. The lord is delighted to receive some traveling players in his home. He enlists their help in playing the joke on Sly. What is the lord concerned about in the following quotation?

   > "But I am doubtful of your modesties;
   > Lest over-eyeing of his odd behavior,
   > For yet his honour never heard a play,
   > You break into some merry passion."

5. One of the major themes in the play is the battle between the sexes, specifically the definition of the proper behavior of a wife. Bartholomew, the page, is asked to dress up like a lady and pretend to be Sly's wife. What advice does the lord give his page that relates to this task?

INDUCTION, SCENE 2

1. In the beginning of this scene, Sly speaks in prose. Toward the end, he changes to verse. What do you think Shakespeare is telling his audience by altering Sly's manner of speech?

2. Another major theme in this play concerns the relationship between servants and the nobility. What services are available to Sly now that he is a lord? Which of these items convinces Sly that he is a lord? Comment on the point Shakespeare is making about distinguishing a nobleman from a servant.

3. Who, according to the servants, does Sly talk to during his fifteen-year dream?

4. A third major theme explores the different reasons a man gets married. When Sly first meets his wife (the page in a disguise), what does he ask her to do? Comment on what his behavior says about this theme.

5. How does Shakespeare introduce the theme of confusion between appearance and reality in the Induction?

ACT I, SCENE 1

1. Why are Lucentio and his servant Tranio in Padua? What do we learn about Lucentio's father Vincentio?

2. What advice does Tranio give Lucentio regarding studies? How does Shakespeare help his audience recognize Tranio's intelligence and education, even though he is clearly Lucentio's servant?

3. How does Katherine's father, in one short speech, upset his daughters, Gremio, and Hortensio?

4. Find an example of a pun in the conversation between Katherine and Hortensio, right after her father announces that Katherine must marry first.

5. Tranio and Lucentio eavesdrop on the conversations between Baptista and his daughters. What does Tranio think of Katherine? What qualities does Lucentio find appealing in Bianca?

6. Who thinks of the plan to present Lucentio as the schoolmaster? What problem does Tranio see in the plan? How is it overcome?

ACT I, SCENE 2

1. Why is Petruchio in Verona?

2. What qualities does Petruchio want in his wife? What does his servant Grumio think about the idea of Petruchio marrying a shrewish wife?

3. Why does Hortensio want to accompany Petruchio to Katherine's house?

4. When Tranio, disguised as Lucentio, declares his intention to woo Bianca, what do Hortensio and Gremio want? What is Tranio's response?

ACT II, SCENE 1

1. How does Katherine's relationship with her father motivate her to continue her shrewish behavior?

2. What names are Hortensio and Lucentio using in their disguises as teachers?

3. Petruchio defines his idea of a proper wife through the adjectives he uses to compliment Katherine. List the words Petruchio uses to describe Katherine.

4. Another of the motifs in this play is to present the reasons people get married. What arrangement does Petruchio make with Baptista before trying to win Katharina's love? Comment on what these arrangements say about a man's reasons for marrying.

5. Animal imagery is also an important motif in this play. Find an example of it when Baptista discusses Katherine's ability to learn to play the lute with Hortensio. What does this kind of comparison suggest about how men feel about their wives?

6. How does Petruchio plan to deal with Katherine's shrewish behavior if she rails, frowns, is mute, if she tells him to leave or if she refuses to marry him?

7. Why does Katherine strike Petruchio? What is his response?

8. What evidence is there that Katherine is enjoying her conversation with Petruchio and respects him?

9. What does Petruchio tell Tranio and Gremio about the way Katherine behaves when they are alone? Why is this tactic a clever move?

10. Tranio (pretending to be Lucentio) outbids Gremio, but the marriage contract is not secure. What condition does Baptista put on the marriage between Tranio and Bianca? How does Tranio plan to satisfy Baptista?

11. Prove the following statement: Tranio is an unusual servant and possesses many of the qualities of a nobleman.

ACT III, SCENE 1
1. How do Lucentio and Hortensio each try to woo Bianca using their disguises as schoolmasters? Who do you think Bianca prefers?

2. What evidence is there that Hortensio is considering giving up his quest for Bianca?

ACT III, SCENE 2
1. What evidence is there that Katherine is hurt when Petruchio does not show up at Baptista's house on time?

2.   Why do you think Petruchio comes to his wedding in old clothes? What message is he trying to send to Katherine?

3.   List two things Petruchio does on his wedding day that go against tradition.   What message is he trying to send to Katherine? How does Katherine behave during the wedding?

4.   What is Petruchio saying about a wife's position in her husband's house in the following passage?

> "She is my goods, my chattels; she is my house,
> My household stuff, my field, my barn."

ACT IV, SCENE 1
1.   Find an example of a joke between Grumio and Curtis when they are waiting for Petruchio and Katherine to arrive home.

2.   Why does Curtis think Petruchio is "more shrew than she"?

3.   List the techniques Petruchio uses to tame his "falcon."

ACT IV, SCENE 2
1.   What oath do Tranio, disguised as Lucentio, and Hortensio take together?

2.   What reasons does Hortensio give for wanting to marry the widow?

3.   How does Tranio convince the Pedant to masquerade as Vincentio?

ACT IV, SCENE 3
1.   In what ways is Grumio loyal to Petruchio but not loyal to Katherine?

2. Katherine likes the clothes the tailor brings, but Petruchio insists they are not good enough and sends them away. Since she approves of them without any complaints, why do you think he refuses to let her have the clothes?

ACT IV, SCENE 4
1. Why do Baptista and the Pedant, who is disguised as Vincentio, go to Tranio's lodgings to sign the marriage contract?

ACT IV, SCENE 5
1. What happens on the way to Baptista's house that causes Hortensio to say, "Petruchio, go thy ways; the field is won"?

2. How does Petruchio test Katherine's submissiveness when they meet the real Vincentio on the road? Does she pass the tests?

3. What news does Petruchio give Vincentio about his son? Does Vincentio believe him?

ACT V, SCENE 1
1. Why does Tranio threaten to have Vincentio arrested?

2. What happens that allows Biondello, Tranio, and the Pedant to escape "as fast as may be"?

3. What do you think the following passage says about Katherine's feelings about Petruchio?
> Pet.   First kiss me, Kate, and we will.
> Kath.   What, in the midst of the street?
> Pet.   What, are thou ashamed of me?
> Kath.   No, sir, God forbid; but ashamed to kiss.
> Pet.   Why, then let's home again. Come, sirrah, let's away.
> Kath.   Nay, I will give thee a kiss: now pray thee, love, stay.

ACT V, SCENE 2

1. After the women leave the room, what wager do the men make with each other regarding their wives' behavior?

2. In the following passages, compare the ways each husband tries to persuade his wife to attend him. Which man is the most successful? What do you think Shakespeare is saying about the proper relationship between a husband and a wife?

   Luc.   That will I.
          Go, Biondello, bid your mistress come to me....

   Hor.   Sirrah Biondello, go and entreat my wife
          To come to me forthwith....

   Pet.   Sirrah Grumio, go to your mistress;
          Say, I command her come to me.

3. Why does Baptista add an additional twenty thousand crowns to Katherine's dowry?

4. In what ways has Bianca changed since the beginning of the play?

5. In the last long speech of the play, Katherine lists the qualities of a good wife. Briefly list these qualities. Do you think Katherine really believes what she is saying, or is she being sarcastic?